TIMELINES INTO THE FUTURE

Strategic Visioning Methods for Government, Business, and Other Organizations

Sheila R. Ronis

Hamilton Books

A member of

The Rowman & Littlefield Publishing Group

Lanham · Boulder · New York · Toronto · Plymouth, UK

Copyright © 2007 by
Hamilton Books
4501 Forbes Boulevard
Suite 200
Lanham, Maryland 20706
Hamilton Books Acquisitions Department (301) 459-3366

Estover Road
Plymouth PL6 7PY
United Kingdom

Library of Congress Control Number: 2007925446
ISBN-13: 978-0-7618-3681-0 (paperback : alk. paper)
ISBN-10: 0-7618-3681-0 (paperback : alk. paper)

This book is dedicated to my husband David . . .

He has made everything possible.

Contents

Foreword

Visioning is an important process for those who want to win in the 21st Century. That includes countries, companies, and other organizations from universities to hospitals to non-profits. If the United States wants a future in which liberty, prosperity and peace are increasing throughout the world, the U.S. must remain a superpower. That requires a vision and a grand strategy. Failure to develop a U.S. vision and national strategy that ensures our superpower status may yield a future where China or another emerging power will dictate to the world including us. Every organization needs a vision, too; every company, non-profit, school, church, and government agency or department, whether they are local, state, national or global. The processes are all generally the same.

This book addresses how to go about developing such a vision and grand strategy.

The world systems we have known over the last several decades have experienced tectonic shifts. Since the end of the Cold War, the changes have accelerated. The future of the United States is now complex and uncertain and the Global War on Terrorism, what the Pentagon calls the "long war" has exacerbated this situation.

At the end of World War II, General George C. Marshall (the Marshall Plan) said, "We are now concerned with the peace of the entire world, and the peace can only be maintained by the strong." (Marshall, 1945)

Although descriptive of another time, these words are as true today as they were then. The United States, the only remaining superpower on the planet is concerned again with the peace of the entire world. Assuming General Marshall was right, the United States must ask itself, how do we remain strong? What does "strong" mean in a world of globalization? And, what do we need to do to remain a superpower as others emerge to take our place?

How does the nation address such complex issues? How can the country solve its problems without a vision and national strategy that looks out decades—not just the next election? How will the country plan for a 21st century world that is vastly different from anything it has ever experienced in its 230 year history?

The nation needs to develop a vision and then a national grand strategy to make it happen *using systems science.*

This book will describe the process that any institution can use to develop a vision. We will look at techniques that will enable any organization or government to shape the current situation so that the future they want to emerge has a better probability of occurring.

Why am I writing this book?

I am a systems scientist. I was first educated to understand physical systems as an undergraduate physics major. When, in my graduate school years I learned that social "systems" were also being studied for their characteristics, I realized just how similar all systems are. Governments, businesses, churches and schools are examples of organizational social systems. If we want to understand the systems we all live, work and learn in, every day we need to understand social system behavior. Visioning and the development of strategies to accomplish a vision require systems thinking.

My career has carried me to many different places working for many different organizations. My first job after getting my undergraduate degree was at a place called North American Rockwell where I was a statistical analyst; very left brained. Then, I worked my way through my graduate program at The Ohio State University where I was challenged to think about systems and their behavior in different ways; very right brained. I had the chance to view systems along the entire continuum of the sciences—from physics to sociology. After receiving my doctorate, I worked for Oak Ridge Associated Universities supporting programs at Oak Ridge National Laboratory. From there, I worked for Ma Bell—back when the country had a "phone company." It was at Bell that I had my first real experience trying to operate on and change a large social system though my experiences at Rockwell, Ohio State and the Federal Government were equally educational. During the Bell System reorganization from 1982-83, I was involved with the Network Switching Systems organization as it split into seven equal operating Baby Bells and AT&T. I do not think most Americans understand what a miracle it was to pick up their telephones on January 1, 1984 and have a dial tone!

The Bell System Reorganization was a life changing event for me. It helped me to understand just what all the theory I had learned in my university years was really all about. There was a lot of "system" in the old Bell System. It really was a wonderful example of interdependent functionality in the best sense of the word. It may not have been as quick to market with new technologies as its detractors suggested, but it was an outstanding institution and a place with a true vision, called "universal service" that drove every action and decision.

Except for my work with the Bell System, it became apparent how rarely we, as Americans ever take the long term view or think through the long term implications of our actions or decisions, or what my colleagues at the Pentagon would call second, third and fourth order effects.

Americans, as a people, tend to be impatient. We think of our strategic plans as being five years long, at best. And, we use the term strategic to mean important, instead of systemic, contextual and long-term. Most of the time, we are tactical and short term. We almost never think of the single most important characteristic of a system—the interdependence of system elements and their interactions with the environment. It is in the interactions of system elements that most systemic phenomena occur so if you are not paying attention, you may miss the most important things of all. Finally, we do not think about why we do what we do and why our organizations exist, let alone, what we want to accomplish in the long term.

Such is the problem with the way most organizations plan and with the strategic management processes they use. Rarely do they begin with an understanding of the system they are planning for and how the system needs to be prepared for the future. This book will not provide a classic strategic management process, there are many already in existence including my own which I will briefly describe. This book provides the piece that is missing from most strategic management processes, called visioning. I hope this effort will help organizations and/or governments develop their capabilities to prepare for the future.

There is a science to seeing into the future or "visioning." There is also an art. This book will explore both sides of this equation . . . the analytical side, requiring the left hand side of the brain and the synthesis, out-of-the-box side, requiring the right hand side of the brain. Some people are good at one or the other. Most people can *learn* to do both. This book will provide a primer for how to look at both approaches to visioning.

This is not a book however, about prediction, but about learning.

Regardless of the models that have been developed to simulate and try to predict the future, as a scientist, I assure you that in the course of human endeavor there is no such thing as predicting the future. The best we can hope for are theories that may describe behavior of systems or processes in the natural or social world that must be tested using the scientific method. Probabilities, not certainties are predictable.

One thing is clear. The more you know about the present and the past, the more likely you can be prepared for the future. That is why scenarios or stories and the methodologies that create them described in this book focus on learning and knowledge creation—not certainty in prediction. This set of methodologies has emerged over nearly three decades of work, but with a scientific history that has come down to us across centuries.

The book is divided into six chapters. Chapter 1 explores what visioning is and why the world needs it—in government, business and other organizations. Chapter 1 also defines what a vision is. In Chapters 2 and 3, the visioning methodology is outlined using two methodologies; the slower more thorough approach and the faster, shorter approach used when time is of the essence. Chapter 2 also describes what it would take to create a complete 360° vision scenario or look at life. The complete ten-step methodology is described in Chapter 2. Crisis on Asimov, an example of the complete process is presented at the end of Chapter 2. The shortened fast process that is a mini version of the larger process is laid out in Chapter 3. An example of the output of the shortened visioning process from my work with the UAW-GM Quality Network follows at the end of Chapter 3.

The book includes examples of output from efforts of The University Group, Inc., the company I founded more than two decades ago, first at The University of Detroit School of Business Administration where I taught "Strategic Management and Business Policy" and "Managing the Global Firm," and then on my own, as its President, in 1988. Today, I still use these processes in my company and teach them to my students at Walsh College, where I am the Director of the MBA and other Management Programs.

Chapter 4 is the Tartan Scenario, written in 2000 to support an effort at Ford Motor Company that was not developed based on the *Asimov* Scenario, but that did use the entire process. In Chapter 5, I will share my work this past year with the U.S. House of Representatives Small

Business Committee under the leadership of Donald A. Manzullo (R-IL) which will set the stage for the last Chapter and demonstrate the need to understand the systemic nature of setting policy.

Finally, Chapter 6 is about my work over the last decade with the Department of Defense (DoD) and the ramifications of visioning processes to the world. I'll also describe the need for the United States to develop a Grand Strategy including a vision through the establishment of a The National Strategy Center that I co-developed with my colleague, Suzanne D. Patrick, former Deputy Under Secretary of Defense for Industrial Policy.

In the Appendix, I describe an introduction to the learning process needed for visioning that I call accelerated learning cycles.

Acknowledgments

There are many people to whom I am very grateful. I have had the honor and privilege of having many colleagues, friends and family who have stood by me even when it wasn't easy. It was wonderful to have loving supportive parents, the late Chadwick and Cema Rakusin who gave me a love of learning and life and the values that have defined that life. I am certainly the product of a public school education, first within the Cleveland Heights School system and then, The Ohio State University.

Ohio State was a great place to learn and I am grateful to Leonard Jossem, the Chairman of the Physics Department in the 60's and 70's who took me under his wing in the Honors Program, David Marsh at University College who was a mentor and friend, and Donald Sanders, my fabulous Ph.D. major advisor whose interest in systems thinking and public policy was contagious and sent me down a path that led me to this day. I must also thank the late Harold Enarson, the President of Ohio State during my graduate years who also served as a mentor and friend, and helped me to envision a future that could be and how to work toward that future.

Many of my colleagues whose work with me is described in this book include Vince Barabba, Paul Cerjan, Keith Cooley, Patrick Cronin, Ed Deming, Jim Donaldson, Bob Dorn, Brad Knox, Jim Locher, Don Manzullo, Suzanne Patrick, Charley Taylor, Tom Walsh, Jay Wilber, Fran Wilson, and Sergio Wechsler.

I want to also thank my colleagues over the last thirty years whose direct and indirect support includes Ken Baker, Patti Benner, Hans Binnindijk, Brad Botwin, David Chao, Pierre Chao, Mark Crawford, Bob Dekruff, Steve Deneroff, Chuck Centivany, Penny Dixon Bryant, Steve Flanagan, Karen Gillmor, Alan Gropman, Paul Halpern, Paul Hanley, Erik Kjonnerod, Lynda LaBarge, Diana Laitner, David Leech,

Kathleen Ligocki, Chuck Link, Ira Lowe, John McElroy, Rod Meloni, Margaret Morgan, Jac Nasser, Bob Polk, Jim Rucker, Nick Scheele, Larry Smith, Marge Sorge, Myron Stokes, Lynne Thompson, Alan Tonelson, Greg Ulferts, and Chris Waychoff.

I also want to thank my newest colleagues at Walsh College, especially Rod Hewlett, who has encouraged me to finish this book for our visioning course in our new Master of Science in Strategic Leadership program.

I must also thank the late Isaac Asimov, Carl Sagan and Douglas Adams who have inspired me in so many ways, as well as the great scientists of the ages from Newton to Galileo to Einstein.

My family has always been supportive. My sister, Barbara Perkins, who was my primary editor, and her husband Don Shaffer; my brother Benson Rakusin, who inspired Benson Chadwick, and his wife Ingrid Fils, my sister-in-law Amy Ronis Vidmar and her husband Dennis, who put me up for years in their home in metro Washington so I could really get engaged in the public discourse. I cannot thank my in-laws, Richard and Miriam Ronis enough. Their love, encouragement and support have no bounds.

My husband of thirty-four years, David, has made all of my work possible through his unconditional love, support and outright help. Our children, Heather Ronis and her beloved Daniel Mason, whose wedding we are planning as I write this, and my son Jason Ronis, and his beloved wife Amanda, have helped me to envision their future, and I cannot thank them enough.

Sheila R. Ronis, Ph.D.
Walsh College
Troy, Michigan
September, 2006

Chapter 1

What is a Vision? Why is a Vision Important?

The Context

Where there is no vision, the people perish.
—Proverbs 29:18

A vision is a description of a future state and the role an individual, organization, institution, government or country will play in that future. For that reason, the future state needs to be, what I call, a 360 degree look at life in a particular time frame. One of the easiest ways to do that is to create a family in the future and explore their life. That way, you usually can see what role your product or service, your organization or country will play in their lives. It is a first hand view of the future, and you can watch and learn.

There are many processes that constitute "visioning for the future." This book describes both the process and a few examples of the output of that visioning process that develops a scenario or story used for planning purposes. I have put together several examples of such scenarios to illustrate what they look like. One of them, *Crisis on Asimov*, will be used to teach the entire process. The others give additional perspective. *Crisis on Asimov* is about the future of the transportation industry. At the request of John McElroy and Marge Sorge, *Automotive Industries* magazine published excerpts of my scenario in the United States and the *Financial Times Automotive World* published a part of it in London. Eventually, my colleague Myron Stokes published it in its entirety on his website www.emotionreports.com. The scenario was developed using a U.S. Department of Defense visioning process which I had the privilege of working on and helping to further develop with the U.S. Army War College Institute for Strategic Studies and the Army's late strategic futurist, Charles W. Taylor. The visioning process in this book can be defined as the series of techniques and methodologies that created *Asimov*. It is used to test assumptions. Visioning should be used as an important tool in any organization's planning cycle and as part of a strategic management process.

Current use of Strategic Management Processes

Most organizations of any size do some sort of planning. Most of the time, that planning cycle surrounds the budget cycle whether in a school, a company, an organization (of which there are many kinds,) or a government institution. This is also true for countries that plan around their legislature's funding mechanism. All organizations are social systems. I will use the term organization to describe social systems of any kind— schools, government institutions, non-profits, countries, etc. Organizations refer to all of them. Sometimes, I will refer to a specific kind of organization or institution, but most of the time I will simply use the term "organization" to refer to any one of them.

Social systems should begin their planning process with some key questions that need to be asked before any planning begins.

- What is going on in the world that the organization needs to know about?
- What is the organization today? What does it do? Why does it exist?
- Where is the organization going?
- How is the organization going to get there?
- What does the organization need to know today?
- What does the organization need to do today for immediate results?
- What does the organization need to do today to improve the probability that the future that it wants to have happen, does happen?

Because few organizations or governments think about these questions, their ability to accomplish their objectives is reduced. That is what visioning helps them to learn. The answers to these questions are enablers to being successful and even winning.

Visioning should always be a part of the strategic management process of an organization. Done correctly, visioning is a disciplined series of steps that helps an organization answer the questions needed in order to be prepared for the future. If an organization cannot answer these questions, it is unlikely that the organization is prepared for the future.

When these questions are explored, strategic management processes are more effective. That is why visioning processes matter even if the answers are not perfectly accurate. *The questions must be thought about in an overt way.*

Visioning

There are an infinite number of potential futures, so a vision of the future is not a forecast or a prediction but a planning tool to think about events that could happen in the future before they occur.

In *Asimov*, it is the role of Benson Chadwick, his wife, Yoshiko, and their two children, Peter and Anna, that are fully explored, with regard to everything. We not only look at transportation, but also medicine, manufacturing, education, communications, business, leisure, food, politics, and the values of the time. You may want to read that chapter first before you read the rest of the book so that the explanations of *Asimov* make more sense.

Although I have been involved in visioning and strategic management processes for years, in my work with the Department of Defense and General Motors, I learned some new techniques about how visioning can help an organization to be more effectively prepared for whatever the future brings.

There are really three major categories of visioning processes that organizations can find useful. Most visioning processes are combinations of one or more of them.

The first process is very short and leads to the publishing of a "vision" statement for a company or organization . . . you know the kinds of statements we all read in an organization's annual report that talks about what they want to become in the next several years . . . like "the leader in transportation products and services . . ." to borrow an example from General Motors. These statements should be used to help communicate where the organization is going to its key stakeholders; its employees, suppliers, unions, constituents, stockholders and so on. Frequently, in industry, the only process used to develop these statements is the PR firm or planning staff that puts together the Annual Report. The process simply consists of someone writing what they think the vision should be or what sounds right and then getting approval from senior leadership to use it.

In Chapter 3, this book describes what the process should be, at a minimum.

A second process can be used to build a consensus with key stakeholders by producing a *shared vision of the organization*. The short or fast visioning process in Chapter 3 enables stakeholder "buy in." It also helps make the vision a reality, especially in large complex organizations such as governmental departments or agencies or large corporations, where whole organizational systems come together to create the ultimate product or service for the customer. But, it is also a technique that can enable learning by the senior leadership together, as a team.

The third set of visioning processes produces scenarios like *Asimov*, and can help an organization to think through alternative futures, and their roles in those futures, by testing assumptions. The complete visioning process description is found in Chapter 2.

Visioning is a planning tool to learn and think about events that could happen in the future before they occur.

There are many different kinds of visioning processes and they lead to many different kinds of results, depending on what you need from the process. Some organizations actually do look out twenty years or more to try and see the diversity of contingencies they have to be prepared for. Some people use scenario planning as a tool to gain consensus or "get to yes," especially to talk about where their organization should go and what the organization should stand for. Some organizations use the process to determine what their beliefs and values are and what they should become in the future if different from the present. At a minimum, values should be clarified and articulated through the visioning process.

Knowing vs. Learning

Every organization should be engaged in thinking about the future with its leadership team.

My friends at the Pentagon say that the really important part of visioning is the process of opening our eyes and minds to things we ordinarily wouldn't consider . . . literally, to "think the unthinkable." It is the ultimate learning and planning tool.

With all the work trying to design and implement "learning organizations," in the Peter Senge *Fifth Discipline* sense, (Senge, 1990) the truth is that many organizations' cultures do not value learning or the knowledge it brings. Most of these organizations have not developed processes to share and use new knowledge acquired. Visioning can assist in this process, but only if senior leadership is willing to learn and use that knowledge. This requires an attitude that there is a need for new knowledge; that, "we don't have all the answers." And, sometimes, that's very difficult for executives to accept. It's what Dr. Senge's group calls getting out of *"knowing"* and into *"learning."*

This is exactly where the Pentagon was right after World War II, when America believed it knew all the answers and before we lost our first war in Korea, and then, a second, in Vietnam and now a third, in Iraq.

Thinking the Unthinkable

The processes I began to work with evolved out of the end of World War II, when Congress asked scientists at The Rand Corporation in Santa Monica, California to help sort through the myriad issues surrounding nuclear warfare. They developed a process to force decision makers at the Pentagon, into "thinking the unthinkable"—what would really happen if nuclear war became a reality? At the time, many in the Pentagon thought they were virtually invulnerable. They thought they would always have a monopoly on nuclear weapons! This thinking ultimately led to the understanding that nuclear war and "mutually assured destruction" was insane . . . it meant nuclear annihilation, and there could be no winners in a nuclear war . . . an important lesson to learn.

Concurrent to the development of the Rand Corporation process in the late forties and early fifties, the concept of general systems theory was also emerging. In this work, scientists began to view the world differently—not just using the tools of analysis, but also of synthesis, which put the pieces of a system together in order to understand the whole. This created a new way of looking at the world using a discipline called integration, which puts pieces together to understand how their fit makes the "whole" work. Ultimately, this discipline evolved into systems thinking and systems science. (Buckley, 1968)

Systems Theory

At the same time that the theories of synthesis appeared, there was an increasing awareness that general systems theory applied to all natural systems; physical, biological, ecological, economic, even social, financial and organizational. (Capra, 1982)

Visioning processes are excellent ways for senior leaders to learn the peculiarities of the social system they are managing. We know that all formal social systems are essentially living; without people, they are nothing but concrete, paper, intellectual property and digital information. As living systems, they are in a constant process of interaction with their environment and their many stakeholders. At first glance, some very large organizations may seem like systems of forbidding complexity. So, to understand a system, it is crucial to understand its elements and their interactions. (Ackoff, 1994).

In fact, Ackoff says "The performance of a system is not the sum of the performance of its parts taken separately, but the product of their interactions." (Ackoff, 1994).

Organizations are a special class of system, called social systems, because they are made up of individuals who come together to cooperate in order to accomplish more than any individual can on his or her own. Because organizations change or move to adapt to their environment, they are also called "dynamic," hence organizations are dynamic social systems.

What this means for an organization is that each element of the organization must rely upon and interact with the rest of the organization in order for the organization to work, change, or move in a chaotic environment, and, ultimately, be capable of influencing, even leading, that environment. This behavior requires the ability to solve highly complex problems, which are best solved, not by analyzing them, but by getting into the next larger system and solving them through integrative mechanisms.

The tools in this book are examples of these mechanisms. They can help to resolve what Ackoff calls "messy" problems. Visioning is an essential tool in solving messy problems and this book provides a tool to help solve them. This tool is characteristic of systems thinking applied to organizations.

The Role of Dr. W. Edwards Deming

I was very lucky. During my years in the Bell System, I came across a consultant to the Bell System by the name of Dr. W. Edwards Deming. Dr. Deming was the quality expert the U.S. Government sent to Japan in 1950 as part of the Marshall Plan to assist the ailing Japanese economy and help them learn the quality principles of the U.S.. Dr. Deming worked with Western Electric to help the phone company build the best quality products in the world. In fact, many people used the Bell quality manuals as the gospel in quality. The phone company back then prided itself that its technology and equipment was built to last a hundred years. That was obviously before telecommunications technologies only lasted a short while and then were thrown away or recycled.

Dr. Deming was the first systems scientist I met in the real world after my graduate program at Ohio State. He looked at everything as a system and his approach to quality was the epitome of systems thinking. He taught his students that "experience teaches nothing." When I first heard him utter those words I thought "what does he mean by that?" Then I found out.

Dr. Deming spent much of his life studying epistemology. He was always searching for the truth. He wanted to make sure he knew what he knew. This brought him to an understanding of developing theories or hypotheses and then designing experiments to test those theories, collecting the data, analyzing the data, using statistical methodologies that were appropriate, and studying the data to learn lessons. Sometimes those lessons suggested some form of action or change to a system or a process. But, if there is a change, it must be documented, with new experiments, new data collected, and the changed "theory" must be tested to determine if it really is better. When Dr. Deming told us that "experience teaches nothing," he meant that only through the proper testing of theories about the world could new knowledge emerge.

Dr. Deming ultimately developed and taught the Plan-Do-Study-Act or P-D-S-A cycle. P-D-S-A is a version of the old scientific method in a newer more industrial cloak. I always call the P-D-S-A process "accelerated learning cycles" (See Appendix) because the process is one that is always seeking out the truth and trying to use the new knowledge to improve something. Then the learning process repeats itself and more knowledge is gained. Toyota is probably the largest social system that uses the theories of Dr. Deming to this day. It is so successful that Toyota has the financial resources to purchase General Motors, Ford Motor Company and DaimlerChrysler on the open market and still be able to capitalize a whole new generation of vehicles. I think the process works!

The Appendix describes the accelerated learning cycles that I gleaned from studying Toyota. You will see that P-D-S-A was expanded into a few more steps, but that fundamentally, the accelerated learning cycles can bring an entire organization into a new paradigm faster than any other process.

Dr. Deming was my mentor. He helped me to understand that the large system strategic management processes I was using whether for the U.S. Department of Defense or General Motors were really macro P-D-S-A cycles. When I began working on visioning processes to test assumptions, I began to view the visioning process in the same way; as a series of accelerated learning cycles that needed to be based on theories that are tested.

As an undergraduate in physics and mathematics, I learned that science was classified knowledge based on observation and experimentation. I also learned about the effect the scientist has on their experiments including biases and what they call "a parallax view" or slightly altering the angle of observation that changes the data or object observed and yields less than accurate results. A good scientist always states his or her biases regarding the experiment.

As a graduate student, I learned that social science experiments, especially the case study approach that I used in my dissertation, was a very different kind of observation from the equation based theories in my physics laboratory. I also found that social science may have used a different set of tools but was no less science . . . just different. It certainly was as intellectually rigorous in thought and methodology. It took a lot of getting used to. In many ways it was *more* difficult because the mathematical language I used in physics was more often than not unavailable to me in my real world laboratory.

The methodologies of visioning are similar to those used by sociologists. Most timelines into the future must pass a "plausibility test." They must be internally consistent with current knowledge and observations and based on plausible outcomes. Testing assumptions then becomes a process of research into the present and past.

Visions of the future need to look at the system as it is currently configured, and, then, what it will look like in many different futures.

As we identify and examine the assumptions about the current system it is gradually defined in its entirety. It is the first step of a sound Strategic Management Process. See Figure 1.1. This includes the external environment, or the forces from the outside on the system; the internal environment; and what is called the stakeholder environment, which includes an understanding of all stakeholders of the system. It is essential that the definition captures the identity of the system as it currently exists, and, then, how it could be in the future.

The internal environment of an organization is very important to define since it is the heart of the system. Every organization should understand the forces at work inside their system, if they are going to be able to think through these issues in multiple future timeframes. This includes an understanding of the people of the organization and how well they work together, as a team, to accomplish the work of the organization. What business is the organization in? Will it even exist in the future? Will it be obsolete? Is it profitable? Is it competitive? Is the organization structured effectively and efficiently to accomplish work or is the structure a barrier? What are the functions of the organization? How well do they work together? What is the organization's overall process capability? Is it measurable? What about process integration, that is, how does the process of one function interface with the process of another?

A crucial element of the internal environment is the culture of the organization. How would it be characterized? Is it a positive force for change in the organization or a barrier to change? Are there formal, written statements of beliefs and values? What does the organization stand for?

How are decisions made? What is the resource allocation process? How does the organization invest in its leadership for future generations? What is the infrastructure that supports the entire organization? What are the organization's unique core competencies that separate it from others? Who is the customer? Who will be the customer tomorrow? Do you know the answers to these questions today? How will all of these questions be answered in the future?

What will the world look like in the future? And, how will the organization fit in that future? What will make the organization successful in that future? Answering these questions is at the heart of visioning. Chapter 2 describes the methodology in its entirety.

Figure 1.1 Strategic Management Process

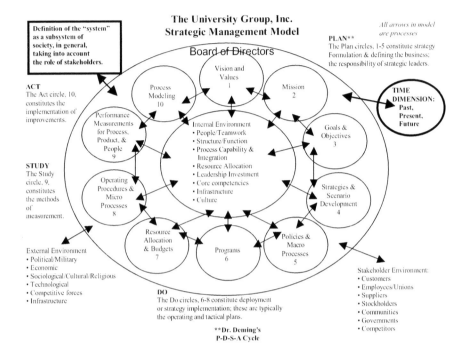

Visioning is a component of Strategic Management. Strategic Management can be defined as managing an organization as a system. It is the set of managerial decisions and actions that determine the long-run performance of the organization in the context of its environment. Therefore, knowledgeable leadership is the key to making strategic management work. Visioning is a way for senior leaders to learn about their system and its future.

Strategic Management has two primary reasons: to help senior leaders as a team to learn, think, grow and make more informed policy decisions about the business *and* to plan and monitor the execution of activities in multiple time frames. Both are essential for an organization to survive in the long term.

Strategic management also produces an integrated strategic plan for an organization. This includes the definition of the organization as a system and a comprehensive strategic management process that ultimately includes a tactical plan, a five to ten year plan, and a strategic process for visioning, and scenario development.

The process is ongoing and therefore, should have no beginning and no ending. Nor, is it a linear process. The process includes numerous elements that must be integrated into a whole. The major elements are broken up into seven major categories: System Definition, Strategy Formulation, Strategy Implementation, Methods of Measurement, Implementation of Improvements, Feedback Mechanisms, and Infrastructure Development. This discussion will describe this process and provide a brief description of Figure 1, the ten circle schematic, since strategic thinking should be the context within which a vision is created.

Circle 1. A vision is a description of a future state and the role that the organization wants to play in that future state. It can be conveyed as the questions, "What will the world be like in the future?" and "What does the organization want to become in that future?"

Visions describe the ideal "state of being" of the organization in the future with regards to their stakeholders; customers, employees, competitors, suppliers, the general public and media. It describes who they want to become in the eyes of these stakeholders and themselves. Scenarios may need to be comprehensive, but vision statements don't need to be long. Three of my favorite examples include statements made by Presidents of the United States. President John F. Kennedy said that the country would "put a man on the moon by the end of this decade and return him safely to earth" which clearly identified the task at hand for America's space program in the 1960s. President Abraham Lincoln's vision for America after the Civil War was that the "Nation of the people, by the people, and for the people shall not perish from the earth." And, Thomas Jefferson, before he was President, described his vision for America in the Declaration of Independence as the right to "life, liberty and the pursuit of happiness." These visions also hint at the strong values of the country.

Values of an organization represent the beliefs and norms that are considered important to the organization or country. Values can usually be represented on a continuum from very formal to very informal and from written to unwritten. The formal unwritten values can be dysfunctional if they conflict with the formal written values! Sincerity cannot be faked.

Circle 2. A mission is the purpose or reason for the organization's existence . . . what an organization stands for, why it is in business, and what it is trying to accomplish. A mission is a broad description of what an organization is striving to be. It should address the following questions in a way that energizes the organization's members: What is the organization's name? Function? Role in the world?

Circle 3. Goals and objectives are measurable and the results of activity. Goals or objectives state what is to be accomplished by when and by whom and under what constraints. These should describe the critical areas for activity and/or improvement for the organization in the next year or two. They must have a level of specificity necessary to develop short and intermediate goals and action plans.

Circle 4. Strategies and scenario development consist of a comprehensive master plan that states *how* the organization will achieve its mission and objectives such as the implementation of "kaizen principles" or continuous improvement in every element of life. "if-then" scenarios should be developed to ensure contingency plans are in place to succeed regardless of the situation.

Circle 5. Policies and macro-processes are broad guidelines for decision-making and taking actions. Policies are like bridges that span the strategy formulation phase to the strategy implementation phase. In order for a strategy implementation phase to be successful, all strategies and policies must be translated into actionable plans.

Circle 6. Programs are statements of actions or steps needed to accomplish a project plan or one element or product line within a portfolio of products or services. All programs must include specific actions to make the programs operational including timelines, people responsible for every element of the plan and their contact information, expected financial implications or physical outcome and a contingency plan if the current plan doesn't work out.

Circle 7. Resource allocation and budgets are statements of all of an organization's programs in dollar terms. They must include all resource requirements such as capital expenditures, expense dollars, human resource requirements, R&D, overhead, etc.

Circle 8. Operating procedures and micro processes are the system of sequential steps or techniques that describe in detail how to perform a particular task. They tend to use process modeling tools as a technique for visualizing the procedure and documenting it at the organizational or product level.

Circle 9. Performance measurements include the methods of measuring the organization's output such as process, product and service measurements. These can range from return on investment, turnover rates, absenteeism rates, defects per thousand vehicles, process control measurements, etc.

Circle 10. Process modeling includes the set of tools used to document and manage the value added steps in the individual's procedures; how the work gets done at the individual level.

Other Model Elements. Infrastructure includes the care and feeding of the troops in the military, or a hospital. These are all the supporting structures to carry on the business, such as telecommunications systems, the education and training of the people, tools to manage the business, computer systems, etc.

Feedback mechanisms include the process of monitoring activities and results so that actual performance can be compared with desired performance and decisions and actions can occur on an on-going basis to evaluate the cycle, learn from it, and adjust processes of the organization accordingly.

Knowledgeable leadership is the keystone to making strategic management work. Visioning is required to enable the learning process. Understanding the system internally, externally and with respect to all stakeholders is essential. Leadership needs to understand their jobs; teaching, coaching, learning, and scanning the external environment continuously to ensure the organization is not surprised by what is going on and in fact knows the environment so well, the organization can lead the environment.

In today's complex systems, it is also important for organization's leaders to understand their integrative, cross functional mechanisms such as integrated product design teams in the automotive or aerospace industries. Leadership also has the role to foster the right environment to encourage learning and sharing knowledge.

The Three Battles

Strategic management processes evolved from knowledge gleaned from the science and theory of war. My friends in the Army teach the concept of the Three Battles. The theory is that all three battles must be fought simultaneously. The three battles are the "near," "rear" and "deep." (Cerjan, 1990).

The near battle can be described as the troops fighting in the field. The rear battle consists of the supply lines, food, and infrastructure that support the troops in the field, from food, water and ammunition to medicine, hospitals and places to sleep. The rear battle also includes the infrastructure that supports getting the troops ready for war from recruiting to training and education.

Then, there is the deep battle. Deep battles are waged in think tanks and policy institutes and within the War Colleges of the Pentagon and academia. Deep battles are battles of ideology and the concepts of wars in the future. The rear and near battles are about the here and now. Deep battles are about the future. The reason all three battles must be fought at the same time is that rear and near battles are fought, won or lost in the current war. If the deep battle ceases to be fought, future wars will probably be lost because preparation for the future ceases.

A few generals who I know have said that even in the most fiercely fought war, a small percentage of resources need to be devoted to the deep battle. Never should all resources be devoted to the near and rear battles. If that ever happens, the chance of losing the current war increases. That is because learning is an essential element of survival within an environment so that adaptation occurs.

Visioning is a part of the deep battle. When we don't engage in visioning and learning, we begin to lose the war.

The Process that Created *Crisis on Asimov*

The process that created *Asimov* begins by asking individuals to think about the system they want to work on. Once the system is determined, the top three assumptions about that system are identified. What I did not quite understand in the beginning was just how much this process tested my assumptions by making me come up with *plausible* scenarios that *negate* each one. And, that is an integral part of one of the key techniques for visioning. . .testing assumptions. When I decided to use this process for the *Automotive Industries* project, I determined that there were three assumptions about the automobile industry that I felt were generally accepted in Detroit. They were:

1. There will always be cars
2. The laws of physics will not change, and
3. There will always be a General Motors.

While the visioning process is being developed, it's important to understand how comprehensive one can be. It frequently is helpful to go far into the future, like the *Asimov* scenario, in 2085, to describe a vision, and then come back from the future to a year ten or twenty years hence. This enables the individuals to break out of their thought patterns, think "out of the box" and accept non-traditional ideas. It is also important to think of the historical timeline and to write a future history as the scenario unfolds. What will the world be like in the future?

In the *Asimov* scenario you will see how I tested my three assumptions about the automobile business. This will show you what a 360-degree look at the future is like and how extensive the work can be because none of these assumptions are true in *Crisis on Asimov.*

Albert Einstein, in the early years of teaching relativity theory, used a teaching tool called a "gedanken" experiment. (SETI, 2006). That meant that he took his students on journeys of the mind in their imaginations to try and explain the natural phenomena of relativity because you couldn't physically travel faster than light, for example, and experiment in the real world. Remember, visioning is also a *"gedanken"* experiment, in the Albert Einstein "thought" experiment sense, because we can't travel into the future, either. Our thought journey is also not a forecast or a prediction, but a way to learn and think about the future so you can do something to "shape" it the way you want it to be. Shaping is the way the Pentagon describes the process of influencing events to create the future you want.

Chapter 2

Visioning Methodology

Two visioning methodologies are outlined in Chapters 2 and 3. The slower, more thorough approach is described in this chapter, and then its faster, more abbreviated cousin is described in the next.

The complete visioning process identifies what it takes to create a complete 360° vision scenario or look at life in a future time frame that is holistic. The complete ten-step methodology is:

1. Definition of your system within its environment or the world situation to be studied
2. Identifying assumptions about the present, especially those considered most dear
3. Creation of a family in the future timeline that you will be looking at
4. Determine what is Plausible: The legacy of Charles W. Taylor of the U.S. Army War College and his "Cone of Plausibility"
5. Selection of a full spectrum of scholars to develop timelines into the future of their discipline
6. Development of a "situation wall" to keep track of everything
7. Plumb lines—describing the cumulative effect of assumptions
8. Creation of a future scenario
9. Testing of assumptions about the future
10. Thinking about what needs to change today to increase the probability of shaping the future you want to create

The Complete Visioning Process

Step 1

Definition of your system or the world situation to be studied. The first step to visioning requires an understanding of the system you want to look at and its definition in space and time. Frequently, it helps to draw the internal environmental variables, the external environmental variable and list all the stakeholders in Figure 1.1. Then, perhaps, the system should be thought of in terms of its past, present and future. See Figure 2.1.

Figure 2.1

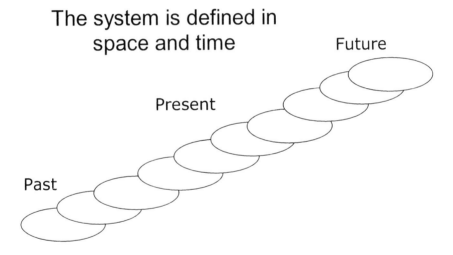

In *Asimov*, the system described was the state of the transportation industry. At the time Asimov was written, I had just completed a three year assignment working with General Motors and thought that I had a pretty good handle on the current state of the transportation industry, especially automotive, at least in the United States, Europe and Japan. My small amount of work with the federal government at that time had me working on projects from the FAA to NASA and the Pentagon. This gave me a wide perspective of many issues related to transportation, but

I decided to focus on the automotive element more in my overall system description.

In defining the system, I began by identifying the large organizations involved, both public and private. These included companies from GM and Ford to Toyota and Daimler Benz to the emerging Chinese and Korean car companies, as well. I also looked at the large aerospace institutions from Boeing and Airbus to Lockheed Martin. And, I began to look at the globalization of industry and high technology from Brazil to Israel, India and China.

I explored the role of government regulation around the world. I had to look at other forces of change—including the social systems that were having an impact on the emerging economies of the world. This included transnational actors other than nation states. And, it included transnational threats such as South American drug-lords, the Chinese mob, the so-called "Triads" described in *Asimov* and even what has evolved into the Al Qaeda of today, although this was several years before 9/11, though after the 1993 bombings at the World Trade Center in New York.

Putting together an overall description of the transportation system I wanted to study was not too difficult. Included are the political, economic, social and technological areas that will have an impact on the system under study. The more complete the description, the better. Institutions need to identify all their stakeholders. In addition, this is where customers, competitors, potential competitors, stockholders for publicly traded companies, and their behavior or that of Wall Street analysts need to be thought through. Some institutions need to look at the role of regulation or legislative agendas. Some must look at the role that technology will play in the accomplishment of work. All globalization forces need to be identified in this step. That includes the potential of work being accomplished away from headquarters, outsourced or offshored elsewhere. In all organizations, external, internal and stakeholder environmental issues need to be as comprehensively understood as possible.

Step 2

Identifying assumptions about the present, especially those considered most dear. Remember, when I decided to use this process for the *Automotive Industries* project, I determined that there were three assumptions about the automobile industry that I felt were generally accepted in Detroit. They were:

1. There will always be cars
2. The laws of physics will not change, and
3. There will always be a General Motors.

What I did not quite understand in the beginning was just how much this process tested my assumptions by making me come up with plausible scenarios that *negate* each one. And, that is an integral part of one of the key techniques for visioning . . . testing assumptions. We will talk about this in detail in Step 9.

Step 3

Creating a family in the future timeline that you will be looking at is the third step in the process. To do this, I went back as far in history as I would go forward. In the case of Asimov, I went back nearly a hundred years. I thought about my great grandparents; where they were born, how they lived, and then, where my grandparents were born and the life they lived . . . then, my parents, and then my husband and me and our children. I then thought about the changes that each generation has faced. I thought about the changes that I and my children's generation have faced. What future changes will my children and grandchildren face? What about my great grandchildren?

My Grandmother, Bess, was born in the 1890s in Patterson, New Jersey, when there were no cars, no planes, no telephones, no radios, no television sets. She lived to see all of those inventions and to see a man walk on the moon, though she passed away just before the emergence of laptop computers and the internet. With the pace of change accelerating, I tried to imagine the life that each generation after me would experience.

I thought about Kiri Tanaka as someone I might know in my lifetime, and Benson Chadwick, as someone who would be in my great grandchildren's generation. By creating a family tree with birth dates (at least in years), the family came alive.

Step 4

After the creation of the family, it is important to understand what is "plausible." The legacy of my friend and colleague, Charles Taylor of the U.S. Army War College and his "Cone of Plausibility" was of great help in this activity. When I first met Charley in 1990, he was the only strategic futurist of the U.S. Army. He worked at the Institute for Strategic Studies, a think tank at the U.S. Army War College in Carlisle Barracks, Pennsylvania. For many years, I had the privilege of working with him regarding my ideas about disciplined ways to study the future. He had developed a concept called the "Cone of Plausibility" in the 60s, 70s and 80s. See Figure 2.2. Charley looked at the political, economic, sociological and technological variables as they progressed into the future of his "World Scenarios." (Taylor, 1990). He separated the future into two spaces or categories, those that were plausible, and those that were not, namely what he referred to as "wild card" scenarios. In those days, the Army expected his scenarios of the future to be very conservative. Even after the Cold War ended, the Army thought their future was mainly predictable, and the need to plan for "wild card" situations was limited. Not everyone in the Army was as visionary as the leadership in Carlisle that supported his work.

Figure 2.2

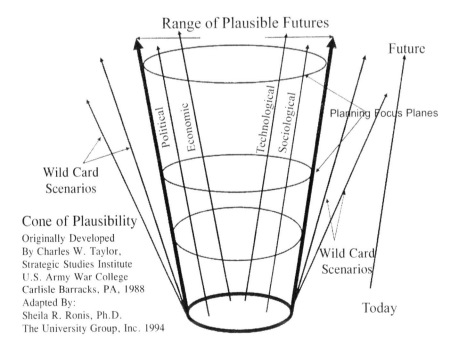

When Charley was working with the senior leadership of the Army in the eighties, they gave him very specific guidelines to work with in developing his scenarios. They were so rigid that Charley felt very constrained. Nevertheless, he was a good soldier and followed his orders to develop scenarios that met the following guidelines:

- The logic and assumptions of the scenarios must be plausible over time.
- The scenarios must focus on issues relevant to Army planning interests.
- The scenarios must include valid trends and key variables that are realistic and challenge traditional Army stationing, training, doctrine, and employment concepts.
- The scenarios must be free of disruptive, aberrant, catastrophic, and anomalous events that would nullify their usefulness for long-range planning.

—From *Alternative World Scenarios for Strategic Planning*
By Charles W. Taylor, U.S. Army War College, 1990 Edition

Being the consummate futurist, Charley developed scenarios that followed the guidelines, but then to ensure he created the scenarios that needed to be developed, he also created many "wild-card" scenarios to ensure the senior leadership of the Army would hear what they needed to know—not just what they wanted to hear. I learned a lot from him. Charley put his wild card scenarios into the very categories that the Army told him would not be appropriate. That is disruptive, aberrant, catastrophic, and anomalous. An example of a disruptive event might be a world wide depression; an aberrant event, a major natural disaster, such as Hurricane Katrina or a major earthquake in a highly populated area, such as the eruption of Mount Vesuvius; a catastrophic event might be a global war or global warming, and an anomalous event might be the rapid democratization of the Middle East.

Charley did not live to see 9/11, but he had predicted something like it many years before. It was a "wild card" dismissed as "unlikely." He had also predicted the collapse of the Soviet Union decades before it occurred in a "wild card" event. The point is that plausibility is not hard to determine in a world of predictability. But, what about a world where the unexpected becomes the norm; in other words, the world we live in? The more likely the scenario, the better it is for learning. And, in order to create a future that is more likely, it is critical to understand as much as possible about the past and the present of the system you are describing. For that reason, an organization needs to be in a state of accelerated learning. For a complete discussion of accelerated learning cycles, see the Appendix.

Step 5

The selection of a full spectrum of scholars to develop timelines in their field and the development of a "situation wall" to keep track of everything. When I put together the knowledge needed to develop *Asimov*, we had few resources to pay scholars for their knowledge of their field and how it would evolve over the timeline of the scenario. With resources, the richness of developing timelines into the future is made much easier. But without resources, I had to develop *Asimov* from work I had done before and a lot of help from my friends and relatives. Fortunately, I had had some pretty interesting assignments from the Department of Defense, and GM. As a fan of Dr. Carl Sagan, the late physicist and author of *Cosmos*, the television documentary of the seventies, I was aware of much of the work that had been done by the Mars Project at the Jet Propulsion Laboratory in Pasadena California at that time. (Sagan, 1980). I was also preparing a visioning effort in conjunction with the Defense Reform Initiative at the Pentagon.

Figure 2.3

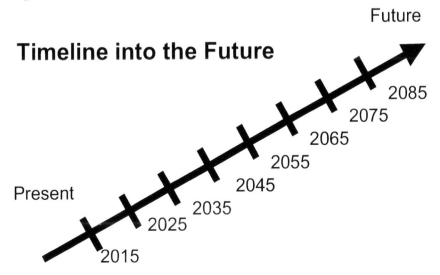

Knowing scientists in many fields, I asked each one to write a timeline into the future to the year 2085 when *Asimov* was written, and describe how their field would evolve over the years in five year increments. See Figure 2.3. I was very lucky to have had many different kinds of scholars and practitioners participate; physical and social scientists, engineers, artists and historians, intelligence and military officers, members of the clergy and educators.

Step 6

I built a small "situation or war room" in my second floor office at 380 N. Old Woodward in downtown Birmingham, Michigan where I worked for nearly seventeen years. I tried to put each scientist's timeline on the wall so that I could compare and accumulate their assumptions by year. Frequently, I just compared them on my large conference table when my walls filled up. Clearly, the Army built war rooms and other situation rooms routinely. I was involved in the building of many war rooms from the Pentagon and the U.S. Agency for International Development (USAID) to General Motors and Ford.

Figure 2.4

**Visioning War Room Layout Timelines—
Cones of Plausibility on their Sides**

Discipline 1	Present	Future
Subject Matter Expert 1—————————————————————
Subject Matter Expert 2—————————————————————
Subject Matter Expert 3—————————————————————

Discipline 2
Subject Matter Expert 1—————————————————————
Subject Matter Expert 2—————————————————————
Subject Matter Expert 3—————————————————————

Discipline 3
Subject Matter Expert 1—————————————————————
Subject Matter Expert 2—————————————————————
Subject Matter Expert 3—————————————————————

Discipline 4, etc., . . . up to as many disciplines as necessary

The development of timelines and a "situation wall" to keep track of all the timelines is the next step in the process. Over many years of effort, I have found that making work visual is very helpful in trying to understand complex issues. In my conference room, I often transformed it into a "war room" to keep track of multiple timelines at the same time to see patterns as they might emerge over many years and within and between disciplines. See Figure 2.4.

Step 7

Plumb lines; describing the cumulative effect of assumptions. In the war room, I would try to make sure that all the timelines were built using the same template or size so that they were easily comparable. I also would use a "plumb line"—usually string with a weight on it to drop wherever I wanted to think through a specific time in the future.

This way I could add up all the specifics in timelines that were occurring at the same time in the future. See Figure 2.5.

Figure 2.5

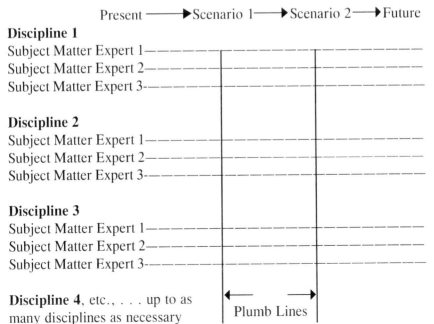

Visioning War Room Layout Timelines— Cones of Plausibility on their Sides

Present ——▶Scenario 1——▶Scenario 2——▶Future

Discipline 1
Subject Matter Expert 1————————————————————
Subject Matter Expert 2————————————————————
Subject Matter Expert 3————————————————————

Discipline 2
Subject Matter Expert 1————————————————————
Subject Matter Expert 2————————————————————
Subject Matter Expert 3————————————————————

Discipline 3
Subject Matter Expert 1————————————————————
Subject Matter Expert 2————————————————————
Subject Matter Expert 3————————————————————

Discipline 4, etc., . . . up to as many disciplines as necessary

Plumb Lines

Step 8

Creation of a future scenario is the next step. At the intersection between the plumb lines and the subject matter experts are the planning focus planes of Charley's model. See Figure 2.2. They are timeframes with multiple assumptions; one from each expert. What I would do is list them together and then look for patterns. For example, in *Asimov*, my hero, Benson Chadwick, is a young man who lives with his wife, Yoshiko, and their two children in a place called Galileo in the year 2085.

As the story of *Asimov* unfolded, each assumption was made by someone who I asked to help build a timeline. For example, Galileo is a space station city that orbits the Earth. There are twelve such space stations, and there are also people living under biosphere domes on Luna, what we then call our moon, and on the surface of Mars.

Saturn is not a car or a car company in 2085, it's a place where scientists travel to; a research facility orbiting another planet in the solar system. In fact, there are no cars as we know them; "to space" is a verb that means traveling in space. There also is no money—only electronic system dollars.

Being a global corporation in that time is considered much too "provincial." Companies, like IBM, choose to locate their headquarters on satellite cities to leave the politics of the Earth behind as much as possible.

Bioelectronics is a mature science, in 2085, but there is discussion about the social issues regarding the use of biological creatures since the materials are "alive." These materials grow themselves, heal themselves and are embedded with artificial intelligence so they are "smart." Many things are made from them. As long as you feed them, they're happy! But, critics believe that there are still lots of ethical and legal questions to iron out. So many people are still against what they call the enslavement of microbes, and even the smartest of microbes has been unable to communicate a consensus of their species. This is leading to the whole debate over the right and wrong applications of science. Things were so easy when there were only nanotechnology machines, but the limitations on them were enough to warrant the development of our smart microbes.

I was able to get input from over 150 people; mainly physical and social scientists, political and policy analysts, and scholars. The only two people who provided input but were not experts in their fields were my two children. When I synthesized the output of all the people I asked to help me put together *Asimov* in the summer of 1997, my daughter, Heather, was nineteen and my son, Jason, was fifteen. Heather was home from Kenyon College and my son was a freshman at The Roeper School in Birmingham, Michigan. They were very helpful, and gifted in the process, in spite of having no advanced degrees! But, the scenario wrote itself once all the estimates in the time period were listed. If they all were to coexist, at the same time, it was pretty clear what kind of a world it would be like.

Step 9

Testing of assumptions about the future is the next step. Once the future is revealed in the description of the future timeframe and the storyline unfolds, then the original assumptions should be tested to ensure that the story unfolds with none of the assumptions being true.

Charley Taylor liked to create future scenarios in which every assumption of an organization was developed into a story in which all the assumptions were no longer true. But those stories needed to be plausible. That requires a great deal of research. Plausibility means that the story can happen in the world we know. For example, aliens from outer space landing on the earth and providing cures for all of humanity's problems is not considered a "plausible" scenario.

The tests for plausibility in *Asimov* required some research to find the obscure physicist in the 1920s who found the Biefield Brown effect in the literature search (Biefeld-Brown effect, 2006). Thomas Townsend Brown had many patents and his collaboration with Dr. Paul Alfred Biefeld at Denison University discovered the phenomena known as electro-hydrodynamics or electro-fluid-dynamics. More difficult was the research it took to create a future in which there would be no cars as we know them and no General Motors, since both are such a significant part of the world we live in, especially in Michigan, where I live.

Removing cars as we know them is not that hard to imagine with a leap of faith that may or may not be politically plausible in the nation's capital but is definitely physically plausible. Removing General Motors was a little different. I decided not to have GM fail as a business. Perhaps it was my loyalty to my friends and colleagues there. With the forces of globalization, and the pressure put on a global entity like GM from Wall Street, it would not be that difficult to have the company simply go bankrupt because of the sheer weight of their healthcare and pension liabilities coupled with a need to maintain their market shares around the world. That has been true since I started to work with GM in the eighties. It may seem like a new issue in 2006, but GM has been shaky since the early seventies when the Japanese invasion began the process of reducing their market share annually due to poor quality and a business model that has not been sustainable for thirty years.

So, I decided to look at a plausible business decision that GM executives had made that went awry. This, to me, was a much more useful and unfortunately, possible scenario. I used the GM decision to massively invest in plants and technology in China. How could such a decision back-fire for a company? Unfortunately, the Triads in China are not made up. Organized crime syndicates in many parts of the world are a fact of life. My friends in the intelligence community thought that the issues of cyber-terrorism were very real threats against the economy of the United States. And many nations' industries can benefit by hurting U.S. companies. For that reason, some countries "look the other way" when their organized crime institutions attack any legitimate business. In the case of the Chinese Triads, however, there is also evidence that the Chinese government has little control over their organized crime institutions . . . from mining to slavery. So, I took General Motors out using the Triads, the Chinese mob, negating my last assumption.

Step 10

Thinking about what needs to change today to increase the probability of shaping the future you want to create is the final step in the process. This requires a timeline to be reversed. When experts develop their timelines into the future, they tend to write a future history, as I did in *Asimov*. Much of Chapters 1 and 2 in the *Asimov* scenario describe what has happened between today and the timeframe of the scenario. In the case of *Asimov*, that timeline went from 1997 to 2085. After reading the scenario, it is critical to ask, "Is it what I want to have happen to me and my family, my organization, my country?" When the answer is "no," there are several things that the leader of an organization must do. First of all, they need to understand the dynamics of what occurred and how it came to be.

The more understanding there is, the more likely a leader can change something in their internal, external or stakeholder environment today to create the kind of change that is needed to stop a phenomenon from occurring in the future or to create a phenomenon that is essential. That kind of understanding only occurs with a lot of learning individually and organizationally, and, of course that is a requirement of the visioning process.

The scenario, Crisis on Asimov, which uses the complete visioning process follows.

Crisis on Asimov

Introduction

Tucked away in Denso's secret laboratory, Nobel Prize winner, Dr. Kiri Tanaka, stared in disbelief out her window at the gentle rolling hills on the island of Kyushu, Japan. She'd just confirmed the Biefield Brown effect is real. From now on, the world will never be the same.

The ramifications are mind-boggling. It marks the end of the internal combustion engine as the only way to cost effectively move people and product. If her analysis is correct, when current goes through a wire, the positive pole is lighter than the negative pole and the positive side is lifted into the air. In short, we can fly through the conductivity of electricity, alone.

She ran over the scenario in her mind. She'd been working on Einstein's Unified Field Theory, which looked for the relationships between electricity, magnetism and gravity. She'd just found it.

During a routine search in this area of physics, she came across the work of an obscure physicist from the early part of the last century, Thomas Townsend Brown of Denison University. In the 1920s, he discovered that if placed in free suspension with the poles horizontal, a condenser, when charged, exhibited a forward thrust toward the positive pole. The scientific community, pushed by the powerful electrical companies, that wanted no part of cheap energy, wrote it off as a fluke.

Using powerful simulations, she verified the work in the computer, since her models were built with all known theories of physics. She confirmed the computer's calculations by replicating Dr. Brown's work.

Looking at her reflection in the window, she muttered quietly, "Now I know what I'll tell the Denso scientific meeting next month. I also know what the future of my grandchildren will be like."

PTVs

Kiri's grandson Benson Chadwick opened one eye. "Good morning Benson. It is July 1, 2085 at 0500, and your PTV (Personal Transportation Vehicle) is programmed to depart at 0600 so you can catch the 0615 shuttle to the Earth. It's time to rise and shine," murmured his alarm clock.

Benson was heading for an IBM senior executive knowledge sharing conference on Earth. His job was to explain to the company elders why PTV consumer preferences are so different on each of the 12 satellite cities orbiting the Earth. He has also been asked to give a psycho-graphic profile of Boris Chin, the chairman of the System Safety and Environmental Council (SSEC).

The SSEC will soon decide what company will win the century's most lucrative PTV contract—to build drivable PTVs for Asimov, a Disney-Sagan resort. For decades, no one has been allowed to drive a vehicle anywhere in the system because of environmental and safety concerns.

In 2021, money the world over was replaced by electronic "system dollars" and currency disappeared. Now, people use Microsoft debit cards throughout the system to buy everything. In 2019, Microsoft, knowing that the movement of wealth would yield the greatest profits, purchased MasterCard, Visa International and American Express.

That was only one of the major changes in the early part of the 21st century. IBM, as it is configured in 2085, was created back in 2020, when the merger wave of the old automobile industry took place as globally competitive companies tried to battle Toyota, CIMMCO, (the China Integrated Motors and Manufacturing Company,) and the huge Ford Sony Boeing Group or FSB.

The system's largest transportation company is FSB. It was created in 2017 when the boards of the three organizations realized they held the required synergies between them for the future of transportation, based on Biefield-Brown technology. Ford executive, Jason Deming, who sat on the Sony board, found out Sony scientists were close to perfecting that technology. With Sony's blessing, Ford scrapped all plans for vehicles with wheels. Instead, it threw all available R&D money toward the development of a global infrastructure and the creation of Personal Transportation Vehicles.

Realizing it couldn't go it alone, Ford approached Sony and Boeing. That merger married Ford's marketing ability, Sony's electronic prowess and Boeing's skill at building lightweight space-frames that integrate sophisticated electronics, such as fly-by-wire and avionics.

During that time, the former automotive industry was becoming the PTV global infrastructure as we know it today, and the need to "space" (a verb) was changing the industry as well. Being a global corporation at that time was considered much too "provincial."

IBM was organized out of what was left of General Motors, Daimler and Volkswagen. After the information wars, these companies knew they could not go it alone and be competitive, so they joined together.

Back in the late 20th century, GM emerged as the dominant automaker in China. It negotiated relationships with every province and every major Chinese manufacturer and supplier so that the Chinese automotive infrastructure and GM became one and the same.

In the late 1990s, Hong Kong was re-annexed to China and Taiwan followed after more than a decade. Those industrial powerhouses were integrated into the old Communist systems of China. By 2007, China, Inc. was created, modeled loosely after Japan's MITI system. Ten years later, China had become a global powerhouse. Its transportation arm was called CIMMCO. It soon became a haven for organized crime.

For millennia there had been a profoundly evil ancient Chinese influence which manifested itself as the "Triads." It wove its way into CIMMCO when the organized crime family in Guangdong province requested a percentage of the organization in exchange for the protection of its employees throughout the province.

CIMMCO obliged.

Seeing an opportunity to hike the stock price, the family decided to destroy GM. If CIMMCO's leadership would have uncovered the family's plan it would have taken steps to prevent it. But the stealth capabilities of the Triads were so superb that there was no warning. The Triads proceeded undetected.

Using the best information warfare techniques of the day, they were capable of delivering viruses into the heart of every major computer system that ran their giant nemesis, General Motors. One knocked out the global design network when five suppliers making parts of the interior for GM unwittingly introduced the viruses into the system. The Triads planted parts of the virus in each supplier's system. When GM linked each program, the system crashed.

A second virus took out the database system that linked accounts payable and the supply community.

For all intents and purposes, GM was dead. So were several other companies.

Prior to the information wars, GM had linked its computer system with other automakers to keep several joint ventures running smoothly. When GM's systems went down, so did those at VW and Daimler.

Desperate to save the elements that GM represented in the U.S. industrial base, the government stepped in. A small Pentagon brain-trust, seeing the potential for PTVs, encouraged IBM to buy GM's remaining assets and sink money into that technology. IBM decided to create a global empire by buying what was left of GM's other partners for rock bottom prices. It was 2020.

What made it all work was the ability to tap into something called the Quality Network process, GMs historic quality process with the United Auto Workers where union and management worked together to solve problems. The Quality Network became *the* process that enabled IBM to manage the new global business. It was perfect to merge the cultures of the three companies, solving problems along the way.

Although it surprised many people, the Quality Network Process survived over the years because it was timeless. It had been developed jointly by General Motors management and the UAW, based on a set of beliefs and values that stood the test of time. The beliefs and values had been the result of an extensive study in which the question was posed, "How should people be treated in the company?" It was a wrinkle of the "Golden Rule," and those fundamentals culminated in a vision of "Customer satisfaction through people, teamwork and continuous improvement."

There was even discussion that the name should be changed, but those discussions gradually evaporated as the phrase "Quality Network" became a common term throughout the system. Its ideals were universally accepted.

In the year 2007 the leadership of the UAW thought the role that they were playing was diminishing along with their membership numbers. As corporations became global, the UAW realized it needed to seek new members in the emerging nations of the world. The emphasis on North America changed to a global view. In the process, they targeted all global automotive OEMs and their tier suppliers. The original union values to improve the human rights of workers and remove oppressive conditions were the cornerstone of the UAW's global strategy.

Countries from Kazakstan to Saipan became the domain of the UAW. In 2015, Mathew Tanaka, International President of the UAW, was awarded the Nobel Peace Prize for his efforts in ending the war between the workers in Turkmenistan and their Russian corporate leaders. The workers in this central Asian nation armed themselves against their Russian employers who were treating them as slaves. Dr. Tanaka was able to eliminate the oppression and end all the violence toward the workers.

By 2020, "cars" as they were known in the early part of the 21st century no longer existed. Their legacy of personal transportation was the PTV, completely driven by computers coming in all shapes and sizes. The enormous global supply base to the old automotive industry was very adaptive. They were able to change over to the ever changing industry needs through their own capabilities, since so much of the transportation knowledge in the latter part of the 20th century already resided inside their companies. The UAW, as well, realized that their new membership around the world needed the knowledge necessary to help the global industry, and their major value-add was providing those knowledge based manufacturing workers. Education and training had become the single greatest activity within the union.

By 2025, workers around the world were represented. Working and living conditions soared. So did the quality of life around the world. It was increasingly difficult to decide who was a "worker," and who was a "non-worker." Almost everyone was a worker and a manager and a leader. As labor-intensive jobs were gradually replaced with machines, every worker was a thinker, a problem solver, and a team player. Manufacturing facilities had an increasing number of workers with advanced degrees. The difference between workers in the manufacturing facilities and senior management blurred.

In addition, governments around the world took America's lead in protecting workers' health and safety. Many within the union itself questioned whether the UAW still had a mission.

The largest supplier to the PTV industry in 2085 is Delphi Services, whose ancient liaison with General Motors had been terminated at the turn of the century. The UAW decided to choose Delphi for an experiment in 2030 to see if PTV modular construction could occur in a Delphi facility with a different kind of relationship with the workers. After all, Delphi assembled PTVs for every OEM in the world. What if the workers weren't Delphi employees, but UAW employees, and the UAW didn't represent the people, but employed them? What if the UAW, in essence became a corporation? Its customers would then contract this corporation for its employees; the UAW's former members?

Over a period of a decade, that was exactly what occurred. The United Transportation Services Corporation (UTS) emerged as a global organization employing all the UAW's former members as well as most union leadership. The UAW, as a union, gradually dissolved. UTS quickly emerged as the world's largest corporation, supplying the knowledge-based workers for the transportation industry, using their wonderful Quality Network process. Although UTS was a publicly traded company, its employees still owned much of the stock and operated the company . . . very profitably.

As part of the original fire sale, IBM sold off several brand names to some Tier 1 interior suppliers. One snapped up the Cadillac name for luxury interiors. Another used Chevrolet for entry-level family interiors.

Along with the PTVs, there were many systems of mass transit throughout the solar system. Kiri had predicted this future the moment she realized the ramifications of her work so many years ago.

All of this history was foremost in Benson's mind as he thought about his day ahead.

Earth

Benson's wake-up alarm always told him what he needed to know first thing in the morning. He programmed it the night before.

"Oooo . . . it's so early. Maybe I had too much champagne last night. But, I better get moving. It's going to be a big day," Benson said to himself.

By the time the shuttle left, Benson was already concerned about how his presentation would go in front of the new company elders. It was easy to communicate in a virtual world, but reality?

Looking out of the shuttle, Benson saw the huge solar satellites collecting energy from the sun. Most of the Earth and its satellite cities use solar energy, including most PTVs and PTV hybrids. Solar energy is microwaved to Earth, and then beamed to power everything on Earth. Smaller versions of these solar satellites power the Moon and Mars.

PTVs move people and their cargo. On the Earth, they move, like hovercraft, over relatively flat spaces. Most road surfaces are green by law since the ozone hole has to stay closed. The bulk of the land mass on Earth is planted with special genetically engineered plants to ensure clean air. It took a few decades but, finally, the ozone hole was eliminated.

PTVs are available in any size—tailored for any number of people up to eight. Each one is uniquely designed by its buyer, based on the almost infinite combinations of modules. These modules come together to create vehicles that are programmed to transport people almost anywhere on the planet, satellite, or moon. It is quick, safe and inexpensive transportation. It is against the law for a person to manually drive a PTV. Driving is only for emergencies. Since this law passed, deaths from PTV accidents were reduced more than 99.9%. Computers make far better drivers than any human.

Vehicles operate on solar power as well as electric energy supplied by electric batteries they carry for emergency backup. The transformation of solar energy into electricity was improved greatly in the 20s, when breakthroughs of efficiencies were accidentally uncovered by the Ford Sony Boeing Group. Since that time, FSB has remained the largest transportation company in the system, manufacturing PTVs as well as most mass transit ships.

Most mass transit is powered using nuclear fusion. Although the use of nuclear fission was used in the twentieth century, its toxic side effects were simply intolerable and all fission use ceased in the early part of this century.

No sooner did the shuttle take off, when Benson realized they were docking at the plant. The new plant manager, Ito Suzuki and several of his assistants boarded the shuttle.

"Chadwick-san," Suzuki said as he greeted Benson. "I never like these weightless shuttle rides, but, I'm glad that you're here. We can visit on the way and I want to ask you some questions."

Benson smiled and slightly bowed his head. He knew Suzuki well . . . one of the best plant managers in the system.

"Well Benson, do you like the quality of the PTV electronics coming out of the plant these days . . . best in history, with the clean, smart manufacturing available on the space station?"

Benson looked at Suzuki and said, "The quality levels are fabulous. But, the PTVs still need some of the design characteristics that my customers are asking for."

Suzuki looked at Benson. "I know. We're still working to keep up with the new technology as it comes moment by moment. Our modular molecular construction is great, but it is hard to keep up with technologies that change every nanosecond. But, you know our bio-adaptation electronics are getting very close."

Benson was pleased to hear that the company was working on the right things.

Before long, they felt the forces of reentry, as the weightless environment they were in gradually grew in gee-forces. The Los Angeles Metroplex Launch Port was now in view. In a few moments, they would be on their way by bullet train to the conference area.

The IBM conference was held at the great Los Angeles Metroplex resort of Santa Barbara, California, in one of the original hotels of the last century, overlooking the Pacific Ocean. Many new resorts on the planet are underground, but Santa Barbara's is still on the surface of the planet, so it is quite a treat to go there.

Living is mainly underground, too, since the surface of the planet is used for growing vegetation to support clean air and food for the population. Earth has had a self sustaining ecosystem for thirty years, since the fifties, when the entire consciousness of the planet improved. Transportation is under ground, on the planet's surface and in the air. Mass transit is prevalent everywhere populations live; both individuals and communities "own" an assortment of PTVs, the product that Benson sells to his many customers.

Benson's presentation to the IBM senior leadership includes his plans for marketing the newest generation of PTVs on all satellites, the Moon and Mars. His toughest customer is the Chairman of the Board, Yukio Kunisada.

Benson checked into his room. He was first up on the meeting's agenda, and he wanted to change his clothes to look more formal. As an expert in on- and off-world cultures, Benson knew that it required considerable research to meet the special marketing needs of the twelve different cultures on the satellite space stations, on the Moon and on Mars. He knew his task for this conference. He had to explain to the company senior leadership that the needs of the unique populations were as different as the variations in cultures on Earth—maybe more.

Even in an intelligent wireless world, marketing and advertising require that data, information, and knowledge all need to be put in context, to understand specific populations and their needs. Needs segmentation is not a new idea. It is one of those old ideas that became popular in the last century.

Benson knows that PTVs on Mars, for example, when used outside of the biosphere dome, need to be able to crawl on the surface of the planet and hold all of the essentials of life. Inside the dome, more traditional PTVs are fine. The same is true on the surface of the Moon, but Lunies expect many more comforts than the pioneers on the frontier of Mars.

PTVs are the essence of smart vehicles. All the customer needs to do is tell the PTV where they want to go and the PTV does all the rest. Recently, however, customers on Asimov want a new feature. They want to "drive" PTVs as a recreation on the surface of Asimov, the space station city that is used mostly for vacations. The requests are very frustrating for Benson and IBM. He knows that the System Safety and Environmental Council (SSEC) won't permit them to meet their customers' needs without a fight. A great political battle is about to ensue, just the kind of assignment a diplomat might enjoy. Remember, humans are not permitted to drive PTVs by law almost anywhere in the System.

Benson also knew that there were going to be many questions about this as he stood up in front of the group that had gathered at the conference. His friend Jim Swenson, introduced him.

"I give you Dr. Benson Chadwick," he said, and Benson began.

"Thank you for asking me to give you an up-date on the PTV marketing issues I am facing regarding the twelve space station satellites, the Moon and Mars," Benson said carefully, trying to read the crowd.

"I know many of you have questions about the situation on Asimov and the SSEC. But, if you will be patient, I will answer all of your questions after my presentation."

Little by little, Benson went through all the research results. He said,

"So, in summary, this is what the customers want, broken down by type of customer and location, and as you can see, we can fill all of their requests with the technology of today."

"Unfortunately," Benson concluded, "the political challenges are going to be far greater than the technological, engineering, manufacturing or marketing ones."

"Great job, Chadwick-san," said Suzuki. "Now we have to all work together to figure out how we can sway the leaders of the SSEC—though I know that will take time."

Kunisada smiled, and bowed.

And, with that, Benson got a nice ovation. It was a first for him. He had guessed right about what to say, in this real encounter with his many bosses. As he sat down, he breathed a sigh of relief.

Galileo

"Has it really been ten years since we were at Princeton?" Benson asked thoughtfully as he looked across the table at his wife, Yoshiko.

"It seems as if it was only yesterday when we met in that Techno-anthropology course," she replied. They looked at each other both remembering fondly their University days together. Here they were, ten years later celebrating their wedding anniversary in their favorite Parisian restaurant, Chez Pierre.

The fabulous restaurant is one of many the couple have enjoyed since moving to the Galileo space station. Galileo is, in effect, a city in orbit around the Earth. Tonight, the weather is very clear as they are passing over Australia. Through the large window beside them, they have a stunning view of the twinkling lights of the larger cities.

Yoshiko smiled, "remember how hard it was in the beginning?"

Benson nodded in agreement. "We were so young and it was such a big decision to take jobs that weren't on Earth."

"IBM offered us these jobs on Galileo when we had only been married a few months." Yoshiko sighed.

"We're lucky, though. We've had opportunities that we couldn't have had on Earth. Of course, the move and saying good-bye was hard, but we have a new life and children of our own now," Benson said, smiling.

It had been hard for both of them. They missed Earth, missed their homes and families, and it was sometimes too difficult to visit. At first, life off the planet seemed like it could be very difficult. Soon, though, they had discovered that it was not very different from living in most small cities on Earth. The biggest difference was that IBM invested a great deal in the recreational amusements and restaurant facilities on the satellite station, mostly to make it an attractive place for people to live and work.

Shortly after the couple had been married, IBM contacted Benson and Yoshiko offering them both management jobs with high possibilities for advancement. The only catch was that the jobs were on the Galileo space station. IBM wanted Benson to take on a large off-world territory as a sales manager. He was well qualified for this work because of his understanding of multiple cultures. Yoshiko was offered a position as an environmental scientist in the same location. Hiring of couples was very commonplace when companies wanted people to move off of the Earth for their work. Opportunities needed to exist for both spouses.

Benson Chadwick was born and raised in Cleveland, Ohio. He was educated at The Ohio State University where he graduated summa cum laude with a degree in Electronics Engineering. He then went to Princeton University for his graduate degree in On- and Off-World Cross Cultural Studies. Like other students who received this degree, Benson prepared for a life as a diplomat. While Benson was at Princeton, he fell in love with Yoshiko Einstein, who had gone to Wellesley as an undergraduate and was working toward her advanced degree in Environmental Science. The beautiful countryside of Princeton, New Jersey was the perfect place for a romance, however, they both knew that the life of a diplomat and a scientist might take them anywhere. Although they were a typical professional couple, they never dreamed of what was to come.

Benson and Yoshiko took the jobs and moved to Galileo, the location of the IBM headquarters. The headquarters were located on the satellite to show the company's progressive side and to eliminate the political barriers created when companies located their headquarters in a country on Earth.

Galileo was a space station "city" with a population of twelve thousand people, about the size of Princeton, New Jersey. It was one of twelve Earth orbiting cities and like many 21st century families, the Chadwicks lived, worked, and played on their satellite space station home. They also had the ability to travel around the inner solar system. People lived on the Earth and its satellite cities; the Moon and Mars, under their biosphere domes; and several other "satellite space stations" that were in various positions throughout the "inner" system and were used for many different purposes.

Each off-world dwelling is unique. The cities of the sky offer people an exiting place to visit or live. Specifically, Galileo is known for its professional zero-gee basketball team, the Gravitons which are the system champions. Galileo is also known for the Galileo Symphony Orchestra, and Galileo boasts the largest off-world music hall in the system. It is also the home to some of the finest in off-world dining options, system wide. Several famous chefs from all over the world have been brought to Galileo for a multiplicity of restaurants such as Indian, Thai, Japanese, Chinese, German, French, Martian, Italian, Spanish, Pythagorean, Mexican, and "healthy old-fashioned American," from McDonalds.

Benson and Yoshiko were celebrating their 10th wedding anniversary. They had two children, Anna and Peter, who were both born on Galileo. Anna was 8 years old, and Peter was 5. Yoshiko looked at

Benson. She could tell he was thinking about work, but she was determined to talk about their daughter, Anna.

"You won't believe the conversation Anna and I had yesterday morning," Yoshiko said. "Anna asked me when she would see me. She was afraid I had forgotten that her concert was last night. I told her we would be there, even though we had holo-meetings scheduled."

"You must have reminded her that the PTV is programmed to take her there . . . she was there early, and the two of us weren't even late," said Benson.

"Of course," Yoshiko said, "and I promised we would be there on time. I don't think she was convinced though. It's just a good thing that our meetings ended soon enough. I wish we could be less busy. I worry that we aren't with the kids as much as we should be."

"Nonsense, the kids are fine." said Benson. "Besides, it's our anniversary. Can't we talk about something other than the kids and the PTVs for one night? You know I'm worried about the situation on Asimov. I know you're working on the environmental impact statement of what will happen if PTVs become drivable. What do you think?"

"I think," said Yoshiko, "that there are other forces at work in this situation. I can't put my finger on it. Call it woman's intuition. But, something else is going on. Maybe a power struggle of some kind."

"I wonder." Benson just thought. It was hard enough to understand why anyone would want to drive a PTV anyway.

Each day, Benson, Yoshiko and the kids travel around in their own PTVs. The PTVs are already programmed for work and school and can have special adjustments for special events like a concert at school or an in-person meeting at an office. The vehicles travel to the school on the station and Benson goes to the spaceport to commute to his office, an Earth orbiting satellite at the electronics plant, like most manufacturing complexes. It rotates to generate gravitational forces emulating those of Earth, like Galileo, itself. That way, people can commute from Earth or any other Earth-like dwelling place without physical side effects from a change in gravitation. The commute occurs under zero-gee conditions and takes about an hour. This is the time everyday when Benson looks at his schedule to prepare and plan out the day's activities. Yoshiko works mostly from her office at home so she can be near the kids if she's needed. But, when she needs to do experiments, she works in the Galileo Environmental Laboratory. She also travels to places all over the solar system to collect data for her work.

Yoshiko wasn't ready to give up on the conversation, "Peter and Anna are both upset that we have to spend so much more time in holo-meetings and PTVs than we get to spend with them on the important things." Yoshiko sighed, "I guess that's the way its always been for working parents."

Benson shrugged his shoulders saying, "I guess so. But you know kids are never satisfied. First, they want their own PTVs, then they want holo-programs, com systems and digitizers. Before you know it, their neuron paths are addicted to the web games, and it gets tougher and tougher to bring them back to reality. What's this new generation coming to?"

Yoshiko smiled. "Benson, if I remember correctly you played your fair share of net games when you were young and you turned out all right."

Benson looked at Yoshiko and changed the subject, "Honey, do you remember Jim Swenson from the plant? He was telling me about this new technology everybody has been talking about. It's a material grown from biomass. It's really smart. Apparently, it doesn't just remember its shape, it actually repairs itself; heals itself. Jim says the Chinese organized crime syndicate, the Triads, are trying to control the material."

Yoshiko looked worried. "Triads. That doesn't sound good for us at IBM."

"No, it isn't," Benson said, "Are you ready? Let's e-pay and get going." She nodded, as he put their pay-card in the slot provided for scanning.

Yoshiko smiled, "You know it always amazes me that the food here at Chez Pierre is just as good as the best restaurants in Paris, even though all the plants are grown in hydroponic gardens, here on the station." He nodded agreeing, "Well Happy Anniversary, Sweetheart."

"Happy Anniversary Benson," Yoshiko smiled. They hadn't finished their discussion about the kids, but she didn't really question that Benson loved his family. What still worried her was their discussion of Asimov, and the apparent increasing role of the Triads.

Luna

"Anna, hurry up!" Peter called to his big sister as they were getting ready to leave.

"I'm coming," said Anna. She was having trouble with her bag, "It's a very long trip to the Moon, and I don't want to leave anything important behind."

Peter was excited. He had never gone to the Moon before.

Anna was older than Peter. She knew the story of how when Aunt Ingrid was a teenager, she had gone to Mars to study the fossils of the primitive extinct bacteria that had inhabited the Martian soil several billion years ago. When she was 19, she had come back to Hiriyama University on the Moon to get her degrees. She longed to return to Mars and had saved up money all of her six years on the Moon so she could go back and settle there.

In 2057, Aunt Ingrid returned to Mars, this time to make it her home. There, she met and later married, Leonard Chadwick, an archeologist, like herself, with an almost equal obsession with Mars. Their daughter, Natalia, was born on Mars in 2062 and was getting married in a week to Ishmael Jackson. He was a comparative geologist on Newton, a satellite that orbits Earth. He met Natalia on a trip to Earth, on his way back from a research trip to Deimos, Mars's smaller moon. The several month trip made for an interesting romance on the cycling spaceship that transports people from near Earth to Mars and its satellites. The two met at the ship's gym, where each was ordered to exercise at least an hour a day to avoid bone loss and to maintain the strength of their muscles in the low-gee environment.

Natalia was also a Hiriyama graduate. She was a robotics engineer on Mars. Ishmael was offered a great job as a mining geologist on Mars, but he and Natalia decided to hold their wedding on the Moon because Martians have difficulty spending time under earth gravity. Also, they had a lot of family and friends on and near Earth who could not visit them on Mars, not even for a wedding. After the wedding, they would begin the long trip back to Mars on the cycling space ship. Natalia and Ishmael would live on Mars where they would both work. Ishmael would study the differences between Martian and Earth geology.

Benson Chadwick called to his kids, "Its time to get into the PTV or we'll be late."

The kids shuffled past their dad and took their seats around the table of the PTV. Yoshiko followed behind them with one more bag, which she stowed under the seats with the others. Everyone took their seats and fastened their safety belts. The door slid shut and the PTV began to move.

Benson was reading from a holo-document for work. He was thinking about the problems on Asimov and how he was going to have to deal with the SSEC Chairman, Boris Chin. How was he going to find a way to get the SSEC to give IBM the contract to make PTVs that were drivable?

Yoshiko was helping the kids with the crossword puzzle they were doing on the large computer screen on the table in front of them. Of course, the PTV did the driving.

"What is a 9 letter word ending in "r" meaning the stage during gravitational collapse, but before the nuclear reactions begin in a stellar body?" Anna read.

"That's easy" said Peter, "It's a protostar!"

Yoshiko turned to her husband, "Benson, can you think of a composer who wrote a Requiem in German, 6 letters?"

"How many letters in Brahms?"

The PTV came to a stop. They had arrived at Brahe spaceport. They walked through to the check-in desk to find out if the shuttles were running on time and to check their bags. After passing by the security robots, the family took the slide walk to docking bay D29 where they waited to board the shuttle. The shuttle ride was only a couple of days long. The Chadwicks continued to work on their crossword puzzle, eat, sleep and play, and in no time at all, they were landing under the biosphere dome of Kepler, one of the Moon's larger cities.

Natalia was staying with Ishmael's parents, Donald and Barbara Jackson, in Kepler. They had made arrangements for the wedding guests to stay at the Lunar Highlands Plaza Hotel; the wedding reception would be in the ballroom. The wedding itself would be in the Kepler Zen Judeo Christian Chapel. The Minister would perform the ceremony. Natalia and Ishmael had written their vows and would recite them.

Ishmael's mom, Barbara, had been in tears for several months. The thought that her son was moving to Mars, a two month trip away, was too much. She wanted to make sure Ishmael and Natalia would promise to find ways to see them, though, realistically, she knew in her heart, that their new life together would not include her and her husband. For her, this match was not made in heaven. It was taking her son away, perhaps, forever. Maybe, after her husband retired, they could take a year or two and come and visit? How would she ever see her grandchildren?

"These mixed marriages never work out. A Luny and a Martian?" she said to Donald, one day.

"Now, don't be so prejudiced," Donald replied. "You know I don't approve."

Natalia reminded her future mother-in-law that through holomessages, they could communicate every week and it would be just like being there. True, it took five minutes or so for a message to come from Mars, and another five minutes for an answer, so that wasn't bad. Ishmael's mom was so old fashioned.

Ingrid and Leonard had left Mars to visit the Moon for the wedding. While on the cycling spaceship, they checked in on their Mars "dig" located outside their biosphere dome in a region rich with fossils. The "dig" was manned by several robots that did all the jobs archeologists used to do, like digging, charting, archiving, labeling and recording. The recordings were made by a system of surrounding cameras that viewed the "dig" from all possible angles, allowing the human archeologists to examine the "dig" from anywhere in the system, using virtual reality programs. The system was called the Scientific Accuracy Virtual Reality System or SAVRS.

"Oh! I'm so excited," said Ingrid to Leonard as she entered the hotel.

"Our work is going so well, and, now our daughter's getting married, and will be back home so we can all be together."

Leonard smiled. He knew it was going to cost a fortune having this wedding where so many people could come. But, after all, he only had one child, and he wanted her to be happy.

"Why couldn't they have eloped on Asimov?" he asked himself.

But, Leonard also knew how lucky he was. Mars wasn't around the corner, and he knew how upset Ishmael's parents were that their son had decided to live and work on Mars.

Within a few moments, they were joined by Natalia, Ishmael, the Jacksons, Benson, Ingrid, Anna, Peter, and other guests in the lobby of the hotel. At one sixth gee, those from earth felt light as a feather and, of course, it made them feel great. Everyone felt great, except Ishmael's mom, who was still teary-eyed. Ingrid assured her that the trip to and from Mars was easy to make, and they would always have a place to stay when they came to visit on Mars. Little by little, Barbara calmed down.

Benson was so pleased to visit with his brother, Leonard. They were always best friends. Benson shared his concerns about Asimov with Leonard. He always had such good ideas.

"The Moon was the best place for our wedding, Mom," Natalia said as she gave her mother a big hug and kiss. She turned to her father and said, "Thanks for everything, Dad. You know we're going to have a great time on our honeymoon going back to Mars. I'm so glad you and Mom are going to stick around here for awhile so we can be alone. And, the next cycling space ship will get you to Mars just a few weeks after we get there . . . we'll have all the time in the world to be together after that."

Leonard looked at his daughter. "You know I want you to be happy. Besides, Mom and I intend to go down to Earth to the big archeological conference being held in Cairo. Then, we're going to spend some more time visiting with Uncle Benson and Aunt Yoshiko on Galileo. The timing couldn't have been better."

Donald Jackson said, "I've ordered the perfect weather for your wedding under the biosphere dome. I spoke to the dome management council and they programmed the system to ensure perfect temperature and humidity. And, of course, no rain to worry about."

The whole wedding party had to be fitted for their wedding clothes. Anna, too, was terribly excited because she was going to be the flower girl. All the ladies, including Anna, were helping with last minute errands for the wedding. There were flowers to get at the hydroponic gardens and Anna's dress needed to be made by taking a scan of her body measurements so the robots could put together a gown to fit her perfectly. Anna normally didn't like having dresses "fitted" as it involved standing still for the scanner, but her enthusiasm for the pretty dress helped her remember not to move.

"And, by the way," said Ingrid to Natalia, "We knew you had something new, something borrowed, and something blue. I promised to bring you something old. Here, on this gold chain, which belonged to your Great Grandmother Kiri, we have mounted, encased in a gold setting, a lavaliere, of an especially beautiful Martian fossil."

By the time they all got to the Chapel, everyone knew this would be a special day. Finally, the time came. Ishmael and Natalia said, "I do," and it was sealed with a kiss.

Benson thought to himself, "thank goodness, some things never change."

Lessons from Venus

"Bonjour, Dr. Chadwick. May I invite you to attend the 84th Annual Earth Environmental Conference for Senior Leadership and present a paper on your work studying the 'greenhouse effect' on Venus and other places?"

The holomessage was in front of her, and a familiar face was asking the question. It was the chairman of her doctoral committee from Princeton.

"Dr. Saint-Germain. How nice to see you. Of course, I would be delighted to," said Yoshiko to her former professor.

"Will you be there?" she asked.

"Yes, Yoshiko, and the committee felt your proposal was outstanding. We are very eager to hear what you have to say. Remember, it will be at the new Paris Hilton. Do you think that IBM will permit you to share your results on the environmental impact study of drivable PTVs on Asimov?"

"Oh, sir, I doubt it. IBM must be very careful about the situation on Asimov. I am not even at liberty to discuss it with you," she answered.

"I understand, Yoshiko. Why don't you bring Benson along with you? We would love to see you, both."

"I'll ask him. One way or another, I'll be there."

"See you soon, then," he said. "Au revoir."

When Yoshiko Einstein Chadwick received her Ph.D. from Princeton University in environmental science, she had a curious minor. She was always interested in the planetary warming which occurred with the "greenhouse effect" on planets, like Earth and Venus, so she minored in Venusian Science, since the "greenhouse effect" was so prominent on Venus and it might provide hints to save the Earth from such a terrible fate.

"Benson, Dr. Saint-Germain called on holo and the committee invited me to give my paper at the Paris environmental conference. He's hoping you'll come, too . . . What do you think?"

"I think it's great. Do you think they may talk about the new materials and their environmental impacts? Because, if they are, I might be able to go with you. We could ask my Mom to come up and watch the kids, so we can go to Earth for a long weekend. I think IBM would consider it worthwhile for me. What do you think?"

"As if you need to ask me. I'll call your Mom."

"So, Grandma Cema is coming to watch us for a few days. That's great! She always brings us fun stuff to play with from Earth and once she gets here, we have a great time," said Peter.

"Hooray! Grandma Cema's coming. That means great things to eat, too," said Anna.

Yoshiko grimaced. "Do you think she spoils the children too much?" she asked Benson.

"No way. That's what grandparents are for . . . I wonder why Dr. Saint-Germain wanted me to come, too? Just because he hasn't seen us for a while? Hmmm."

Yoshiko asked for the complete conference guide over holo, and it was transmitted within moments.

"Guess who is going to talk about the recycling of nanotechnological robots that have done their jobs collecting toxic waste from cites on the Earth? Mary Beth Livingstone. Remember her? She was one of your professors at Ohio State. I heard she is doing some very interesting work in that arena."

"Gee, I haven't seen her for years. Is there an image?" said Benson.

"Wow. She looks great. Hasn't aged a day," Yoshiko added.

Benson nodded.

"And look who else is speaking! Jim Swenson is making a presentation on those smart materials he was talking about. Funny. He never said a word to me about the fact that he was doing this. I wonder if he knows you will be presenting?"

Yoshiko was sure that Benson was coming.

"Listen to the description of his presentation,"

"Bioelectronics is a mature science, today. Now that most of the social issues regarding the use of biological creatures have been resolved, today's materials are 'alive.' They grow themselves, heal themselves and are embedded with artificial intelligence so they are 'smart.' Most things, including all vehicles, are made from them. As long as you feed them, they are happy! There are only a few known environmental issues associated with the recycling of the bioelectronics materials, and this presentation will explore them."

"He's lost his mind, Yoshiko," Benson said.

"There are still lots of ethical and legal questions to iron out. So many people are still against the enslavement of microbes, and even the smartest of microbes has been unable to communicate a consensus of their species."

Yoshiko nodded, saying, "I know."

"It has led to the whole debate over the right and wrong applications of science." Benson said. "You bet I'm coming to the conference . . . if for no other reason than to help Jim."

Benson sent a holo message to Jim Swenson. "Just thought I'd let you know that I'm going to attend the Paris environmental conference to hear Yoshiko's presentation. Saw your presentation write-up. How do you expect to deal with the controversy? This may not be a good time . . . as you know, we are in the middle of a major problem on Asimov."

Jim Swenson came over holo. "Well, the company asked me to make the presentation and tell our side of the story. You think I'm going to have lots of problems?"

"Yes." said Benson. "But, as long as you're prepared, I guess we'll be all right. But, if it's too controversial, it may effect our situation in dealing with the SSEC on Asimov, where we are hoping to get the lucrative contract to develop and manufacture drivable PTVs."

"Don't worry, Benson." said Jim. "I've handled the worst of the MRM (Microbe Rights Movement,) and I'm sure I'll survive this one."

Days later, as the conference began, Dr. Saint-Germain rose to introduce Yoshiko.

"Today, I have the pleasure to introduce my colleague, Dr. Yoshiko Einstein Chadwick. Her pioneering work in the 'greenhouse effect,' has enabled scientists today to make quantum leaps in reversing those effects on Earth. May I present Dr. Chadwick."

Yoshiko began,

"In the last century, the realities of Venus became evident. For many years, people thought of Venus as a sister planet to the Earth; similar in size, and, perhaps, similar in the atmosphere that surrounded it. But, as the decades of the last century unfolded, and the research mounted, it became very clear what Venus was really like. A rocky surface that is very, very hot—480 degrees Centigrade—almost five times hotter than the temperature required to boil water on Earth. The atmosphere is crushing; 90 times the pressure people on Earth feel from their atmosphere. The Venusian atmosphere is composed of 96% carbon dioxide. There are other gas traces in the atmosphere, but, the famous clouds of Venus, which people have seen for centuries, are not like clouds on the Earth. The clouds are made up of a concentrated solution of sulfuric acid with a little bit of hydrochloric acid and hydrofluoric acid. Not a nice place to visit, and certainly not a place where people would like to live. Certainly not like a sister to the Earth."

She continued, "Unfortunately, man made chemicals in the last century, and various kinds of pollution, coupled with the devastating effects of deforestation of much of the Earth, especially its rain forests, began to produce the potentially catastrophic 'greenhouse effect.' When left unchecked these began to produce Venus-like effects on Earth. The rain in many places on the planet turned acidic, and forests began to die. In fact, there was some evidence to suggest Earth as an eco-system would die completely, as species began to become extinct at ever increasing rates."

"Fortunately, by the later part of the last century, corporations began to understand the role they had to play to arrest the situation. They began by working with governments instead of against them, to make it profitable to do things that were good for the environment. It was hard work as well as expensive to make industry clean, but this work is crucial and must be kept up at the stringent levels at which it now exists in order to continue to keep the environment of the Earth one which will remain a healthy and safe one for future generations. Today, the people of Earth can breathe a sigh of relief because there is little cause for alarm. The fragile eco-system of the Earth is alive and well."

Yoshiko outlined all her recent work on Galileo, and how the study of artificial environments on satellites and biosphere domes was adding to the understanding of the science.

". . . And, in conclusion, I thank Venus. It has taught us much about the Earth and how to keep it healthy for generations to come."

To her surprise, people had lots of questions and comments. Even Benson thought it was interesting.

The whole conference had been great. Jim's presentation was masterfully done. The IBM position was well received. It helped that the microbial spokesperson had much to say that was positive about the wonderful way microbes live in the IBM environment. And, fortunately, nobody asked about the situation on Asimov.

Paris was lots of fun, too, and the food tasted just as good or even better than Chez Pierre!

"Fred"

Yoshiko was on Asimov, studying the environmental impact of drivable PTVs. Benson had to look after the children. Fortunately, they would be at the Virtual Reality Center (VRC) all day. He had lots of work to do. How would he convince the SSEC to permit IBM to develop and build the drivable PTVs?

As he thought about the many challenges, he heard Anna and Peter run to the PTV.

"Bye, Dad," said Anna. Benson heard the PTV talking to the children.

"Good Morning. Your PTV is programmed to take you to the VRC (Virtual Reality Center) for your field trip today with the rest of your class . . . travel time, three minutes and twenty-seven seconds," said the PTV console as Anna and Peter entered the PTV and fastened their safety belts. Anna had nicknamed the PTV announcer, "Fred."

"Thanks, Fred," said Anna.

"Anna, why do you talk to that thing?" Peter asked. "It's not alive, so why bother?"

"Because, he feels alive to me, and I like him," said Anna.

"It isn't even a him. It's a synthesized voice. You're crazy."

"Well," said Anna. "I may be crazy, but I have one more friend that you have. I have Fred as my friend, too."

By the time the two had stopped bickering, Fred announced, "Welcome to the VRC. Hope you had a pleasant ride. I shall wait for you, here, to take you back home. Have a wonderful day."

"Good-bye Fred. You have a pleasant day, too," Anna said sticking her tongue out at Peter.

"Good morning, Anna and Peter," said Jean-Paul Valdez. "Come on in and have a seat at your learning station so we can begin. We're going to Saturn, today, and we need to get started."

Jean-Paul Valdez was a typical off-world teacher. He had lived on several different satellites and had spent time living on the Moon, on Mars, and on the Earth. His job was to help his students augment their technical education with the socialization process which research had proven was essential to develop healthy and happy children. This required bringing the students together, face to face, with much interpersonal dynamics, since their formal technical education was usually done in their homes via the satellite network. Without the opportunity to communicate with one another, children did not learn to build relationships, and relationship building was a crucial element of learning. Another element of Jean-Paul's job was to help students integrate the lessons they learned to other lessons, and show how their work related to life. This was the learning process that had been perfected over the years.

In the year 2007, a group of United States universities, who called themselves the "Big Ten," partnered with the Microsoft Satellite Network to produce the capability to obtain a university degree anywhere on the planet's surface from any one of their institutions through a "distance learning" virtual process. They were all land grant colleges and in the spirit of teaching the masses, decided it was their fate to teach the masses of the world. It was a giant success beyond anyone's expectations. In fact, by 2025, the increased level of global consciousness changed the face and history of the world. The same Microsoft Satellite Network permitted students on the satellites, the Moon and Mars to learn from the great masters, wherever they are.

In the first twenty years of operation, two billion people on the planet received educations from the "Big Ten" Microsoft Global Educational Satellites, and in the process, adopted the values of peace, prosperity, and freedom for all, around the world. As the general population of the planet became better educated, the world population gradually declined, so that by the year 2067, the population of the planet was again at the levels of the turn of the century. In addition, the people of the planet were so involved in creating value, increasing living standards, and working on the "real" challenges, like eliminating illiteracy and global warming, that war-like conflicts also steadily declined. By 2085, there is almost a total peace on the planet.

One graduate student team in India, in 2022, worked on a way to attack the problem of famine in the world. Using the systems theories of the great American statistician, Dr. W. Edwards Deming, and with some assistance from several corporate partners, they found unique solutions so that famine was almost wiped out through better global management of resources. This required global thinking that integrated non-linear solutions by looking at population control, education, distribution of food, political maneuvering and improved genetic engineering principles as a single complex adaptive system.

Genetic engineering was being explored for its benefits to mankind by many different global teams composed of representatives of all major stakeholders. These teams included students, industry experts, government officials, university scientists, religious leaders, and medical professionals who came together to create mutually acceptable terms for the legislation of this new technology.

Genetic engineering of peoples' personality characteristics is prohibited by global law. However, it is permitted for the elimination of most diseases. The average life expectancy of the general population has soared to 115. Since people live so long, they no longer have the attitude that permits the "next generation" to solve a problem they created. Generations experience the consequences of their decisions. People also work in careers that last for eighty years. Because so much knowledge changes continuously, life-long learning is a major activity of most working adults. The formal education of children begins at birth, and continues until about the age of 25. Then, the life-long learning process kicks in.

Anna and Peter like to do their lessons on their own personal schedules, so classes with Jean-Paul, which have to be scheduled, are inconvenient. Even so, Anna and Peter have a great time in his classes. Anna also loves virtual books. Books made of paper are not obsolete. Many people still prefer to read from a printed page, as opposed to an illuminated screen. This is especially true for children. But, most books are not made of paper, but a digitized reality that enables the reader to read and feel the v-book (virtual) as though it were made of paper. The children have seen real books in the museums on the earth, but they couldn't tell the difference between v-books and the real thing.

The only paper book the Chadwicks own, was a gift from the Minister of their Zen Judeo-Christian Chapel. He presented them with a Zen Bible of the Old and New Testament and The Reformation Scriptures. It is cherished by all the family.

"Today, we're going to take a trip to Saturn. It will be a lot of fun. Who can tell me something about the planet we're going to visit via VR? Franklin Jones?"

Franklin Jones smiled. He considered himself the best student in the class. All the others moaned as Franklin began to speak.

"Saturn is the sixth planet from the sun. Saturn has the lowest mean density of all the planets, which means it is very light weight. Its rings are famous, and were first really seen by Galileo. The rings are made up of particles, though the rings are very thin. Saturn also has many natural satellites, or moons, and one major man-made satellite, called Maxwell, where scientists are studying the Saturn System. Some of the names of its moons are Phoebe, Iapetus, Hyperion, Titan, Tethys, Dione, Rhea, Enceladus, and Mimas. Its revolution period is . . ."

"Thank you very much, Franklin," Jean-Paul said, "Would anyone else care to add something else?"

Anna's hand went up.

"Yes, Anna?"

"My mother once told me that Saturn was so light that if there were a large enough ocean, you know, like they have on Earth, only bigger, Saturn would float!" she said.

"Your mother is right, Anna. Let's go there, now, and see what it would be like to study Saturn if we were on Maxwell. Professor Satori, are you there? The children would like to ask you some questions. Children, this is Professor Yukio Satori, who will take us on a tour of Maxwell, and show us Saturn, up close."

Professor Satori was pleased that he had been asked to participate in this project. He believed the future of the solar system, and his work in it, depended on the attitude of the next generation toward the kind of work they were doing on Maxwell. For that reason, he took every opportunity to participate in VR interactive presentations.

"Professor Satori," asked Peter, "What would it be like living on the surface of Saturn? Would it be like living on the Moon?"

Professor Satori smiled. "Oh, no, my friend. It would not be like living on Earth's Moon, because we do not believe there is any surface; mainly gases of an atmosphere, mainly hydrogen and helium, the lightest gases of all. But, Saturn has many moons that do have surfaces and where biosphere domes might be built. Let's take a tour of the rings. Stand by."

As Anna and Peter looked out over the vast particle rings, they were very excited. When the VR program ended, the children whined, "Do we have to come home?" It had been a great experience and they had learned a lot.

"Remember, we're not taking a VR trip, but a real one next, to Earth. See you in two days, and remember, the trip will last five days. I have all the necessary permissions from your parents. Peter and Anna's mother, Dr. Yoshiko Chadwick, will be completing an assignment on Asimov and will be joining us as a chaperone, along with Ariel's parents, Drs. Sophocles and Antigone Saris. We are visiting the Smithsonian Institution in Washington, DC, the capital of the United States of America. Don't forget your lesson to prepare you." said Jean-Paul.

Anna got to Fred first. "Would you take me to Saturn, Fred?" she asked the PTV console.

"So sorry, Anna. I cannot take you to Saturn. That is an off-Galileo trip, and I am not able to leave our lovely home. But, perhaps, one day, you can catch a cycling space ship there?"

"Then I suppose you must take me home."

"Not without Peter. Ah, here he comes. Travel time, three minutes and twenty-seven seconds," said Fred.

"Think it would be exciting to live on Maxwell, Peter?"

"I think it would be boring. There's no planet close by to stand on . . . and so far away. I like living where we do. But, if *you* want to go there and live, I wouldn't mind," said Peter.

"You'd miss me if I left," said Anna.

"No, I wouldn't. But Fred would," said Peter.

"Have a wonderful afternoon," said Fred, as the children left the PTV.

"Good-bye, Fred," said Anna, as she pushed her brother gently.

"Dad . . . Anna pushed me."

"He started it."

Benson knew the kids were home. He wished he had had more time to work. He still wasn't sure what would need to be done on Asimov. He was leaving on vacation soon, and was hoping somehow it would all be settled by the time he got home.

Crisis on Asimov

"Staying at the Disney-Sagan Resort on Asimov must be the greatest vacation, ever," said Peter.

"Well, the weather is always perfect, the food is always great, and non-fattening, and the rides are always fun," Yoshiko answered. "The trees and flowers are amongst the most beautiful in the system. They are meant to be as extraordinary as the most famous English gardens or the gardens of Versailles, in France. And, to some of us, sitting in a garden provides a wonderfully restorative feeling. Our little garden at home isn't the same."

In the middle of the century, plans began for Astro-Disney and its merger with the Sagan Resorts. A new Star Wars began; not a political war, but, a competition in which companies were going to be able to get contracts for the best spots on the satellite cities.

"Are we really going?" asked Anna.

"Yes, your trimester break is coming up and Dad and I think we could all use a little R & R,. especially with all the work on the Asimov project" Yoshiko smiled.

Anna and Peter looked at each other, "We're going to Astro-Disney! Hoorah!"

The kids hadn't been so excited in ages; not since Grandma Cema took them to Sea World for the first time on Earth.

When the break came, they all packed their bags and got into the PTV to go to the spaceport. The family sat around the table looking at brochures on the viewscreen, planning what they were going to do while they waited to arrive. The shuttle ride was only about 50 minutes and the family took a tunnel train from the spaceport to the Disney-Sagan resort.

The suite had 3 small bedrooms, two bathrooms, a cozy living room with a 3 meter view screen, and a small kitchen area.

"This is going to be wonderful." Anna was glad she didn't have to share a room with Peter, and she was going to get to ride the new Space Mountain. Peter agreed, "I want to see Mickey and I want to drive a PTV!"

Benson shook his head from side to side. "Lets get settled in first, Peter. We have two weeks. I'm sure you'll get to see Mickey soon enough. And, you know, driving PTVs is against the law."

"But, you're going to fix that, Dad. I want to stay here forever."

"You know, we can't. Asimov is the only satellite that does not have Earth's gravity. It is deliberately set to make people feel light and happy, so you can't stay here too many weeks before you have to go back to a full gravitational environment, on a satellite, on Earth, or a spaceship. It's probably better, though. If we stayed here too long, we'd run out of money . . . and it's up to the SSEC whether PTVs will be driven, here. Not me."

It was a great day. The kids were exhausted even in the lighter gravitational environment. Yoshiko looked at Benson,

"Well, I'm tired. The kids are already asleep. And, I'm going to sleep, myself. By the way, there's a private holomessage for you."

"Chadwick-san," the holomessage said.

Benson recognized the bowing image, at once. It was Kunisada!

"I need your help. We have a crisis on our hands, and your skills as a diplomat are crucial to the survival of IBM. Yes, the very survival of the company is at stake. How this situation got so out of hand is beyond me. But, now that it has, we must act quickly."

"My friend, this is the situation. I, myself, have just learned the truth," he said.

"When Asimov was built, my predecessor, the late Merrill B. Sands, the Chairman of IBM, bribed the Chairman of the System Safety and Environmental Council, (SSEC) unbeknownst to anyone in the company.

In the process, IBM broke dozens of laws in the System. We could be ruined. Our stock could plummet on the System Exchange. Of course, Sands wanted the SSEC Chairman to permit PTV driving on the satellite's surface, but as you know, that will take all kinds of exemptions, and usually, that kind of contract will only go to one company. At the time, IBM did not have the technology that we have today. So nothing happened."

"The Chairman of the SSEC, today, is Boris Chin. He wants the exemptions to go to CIMMCO (the China Motors and Manufacturing Company); not IBM, and, I believe he knows about the bribe of his predecessor, the late, Martin Garcia. Even though he knows the best technology for this project in the entire system now belongs to IBM, we have reason to believe he plans to use the bribery situation against us to help CIMMCO, as you Americans would say, 'kill two birds with one stone.' CIMMCO does not have the necessary technology. Why they want to punish us for the sins of a prior generation is beyond me, except for the politics, of course . . . and the profits."

"The SSEC is meeting on this issue, tomorrow, on Asimov. I am so sorry to interrupt your family's vacation, but, you are already there, and we need your help. We need to keep this out of the press, and we need you to talk to Chin and talk him out of this action before too much damage is done. Chin is an honorable man which is why I am puzzled. I think his actions may be out of fear of some of the Chinese organized crime figures, who hold stock in CIMMCO. They may have tried to persuade him to go with CIMMCO, to increase the value of their holdings. Perhaps, if we can find a way for him to do the right thing, and save face with his peers? I'm counting on you. If I come to Asimov, it will draw too much attention to this situation. Please call me in the morning on private holo and we can plan our strategy. Thank you, Chadwick-san."

Benson was stunned. How could he possibly convince Chin? He was so tired from the full day, he knew he'd better get some sleep. He would break the bad news tomorrow morning to Yoshiko and the kids. And, then, he would call Kunisada.

After breakfast, Yoshiko took the children to visit Mickey. "Good luck, Sweetheart. We're all counting on you," she said, as they waved good-bye.

Now, he was alone. It was time to call Kunisada.

"Kunisada-san. I received your message last night. Do you have any ideas or a plan?" Benson asked.

"Not really, Chadwick-san. Only what I suggested in my holo. What about you?" Kunisada answered.

"Well, sir, I think I may have the answer. But, only because it is CIMMCO who is our major competition. If we were up against Toyota or the Ford Sony Boeing Group, we wouldn't have a prayer."

Benson continued.

"You know our technology is far superior to CIMMCO's. We could make a major issue of this if they choose CIMMCO, especially since it is our safety and environmental technology that are the best in the world. Toyota and Ford have better technology in other areas, but when people are on vacations, they are concerned about safety and the environment—the strengths of IBM. CIMMCO is still catching up in all these areas. I promise you, Kunisada-san. We have a chance."

"Good luck, my friend. Let me know how things are going. Sayanara, Chadwick-san."

Benson asked the resort's computer how to reach and leave a message for Mr. Chin, Chairman of the SSEC. It said,

"Chairman Chin. I am Benson Chadwick. I have been asked by Yukio Kunisada, Chairman of IBM to speak with you about a matter that is most urgent. Please contact me, here, at the resort. Thank you for your kind consideration in this matter."

Within an hour, Benson received a response. Chin would see him in one hour.

The two met in Chin's suite.

"Mr. Chin, I am so pleased that you would take the time to meet with me," Benson said, as he walked into the suite, and shook Chin's hand.

"I am delighted, Mr. Chadwick. To what do I owe this honor?"

"I will not mince words," said Benson. "IBM, as you know, would like to receive both the exemption, and the contract to produce a generation of PTVs which can be driven on Asimov's surface. We believe we have the best technology available, and we are prepared to do whatever is necessary to convince whomever we need to that we should receive this contract."

"We are also familiar with the political pressure on you to award CIMMCO this contract by using the situation of our former Chairman's wrongdoing, though that is ancient history, and no one alive today, was even involved. Please understand, sir, that if CIMMCO were to be awarded this contract, IBM will have to call for a formal investigation of the SSEC, and I believe this could negatively reflect on you and your honorable Council. Perhaps, those putting pressure on you would understand how much damage this could cause them, as well? IBM wants to see the right thing done, and you are an honorable man. There is a strong possibility that CIMMCO can receive a small portion of the contract from us to make those sections of the PTVs that are their strength. Is there anything we can do to help?"

Benson was trying to minimize the effect of the Sands issue. He needed to make Chin aware that giving CIMMCO the whole contract would not be viewed favorably by anyone in the system. They just did not have the appropriate technology.

Chin was surprised at how much Benson knew. He was not aware that IBM knew he knew about the Sands situation, and he was shocked that they knew about the syndicate. He was totally unprepared, though he was relieved. Now, he could do the right thing for safety and the environment without causing any negative consequences. He also had what he needed to convince the syndicate that they would be in trouble if CIMMCO got the entire contract, yet could tell them CIMMCO could get a piece of the action . . . one they could handle.

"Why, Mr. Chadwick. What makes you think there is a problem with the SSEC awarding the contract to IBM? We intend to give IBM the award today. I am so pleased you will be here to tell your chairman of our findings. Please come to our meeting. It is at 1400 this afternoon, here at the resort. Will you join me and some of the other Council members for some lunch?"

Benson smiled. His approach worked. Chin was an honorable man. The Council would give IBM the exemptions and contract they needed with no problems, and Chin would let the Chinese syndicate know the damage he was able to avoid on their behalf. It was truly the win-win situation Benson and Chin had hoped for.

After the meeting, Benson sent his holomessage.

"Kunisada-san. IBM has received the exemptions and contracts to prepare drivable PTVs on Asimov. All problems were averted.

"How did you persuade him, Chadwick-san?" Kunisada asked.

"Chin is an honorable gentleman." Benson explained. "I have learned in my studies of many cultures and organizations that the secret of diplomacy is making everyone satisfied with the final agreements.

"More than 2600 years ago, a Chinese philosopher Sun Tzu, wrote in a book called, *The Art of War*,

'If you know the enemy and you know yourself, you need not fear the result of a hundred battles. If you know yourself but not the enemy for every victory gained, you will suffer a defeat. But, if you know neither yourself, nor your enemy, you will succumb in every battle.'

"I knew about all the parties involved. And, I knew us. Perhaps, today, we should call Sun Tzu's philosophies, the art of peace."

"Chadwick-san," said Kunisada. You have a wonderful vacation with your family. I want you to know that this situation could have been catastrophic to the company. Your courage and knowledge will not go unrewarded. When you return to work, you will find you have been promoted to Vice President. On behalf of the company, I congratulate you."

Benson knew it would be a great holiday!

Timeline for the Asimov Scenario developed in the summer of 1997 . . .

2002   Microsoft and Samsung begin working together

2005   Microsoft and the Big 10 use satellite network to educate people around the world

       China, Inc. emerges; CIMMCO is created

2010   Ford absorbs Mazda

       BMW/Honda/Chrysler merge

2012   Biefeld-Brown theory proven in Japan, but entire world races to commercialize it, which Ford ultimately wins

       English, Chinese and Spanish emerge as the world's major languages

2015   Mercedes and Cadillac merge as the "ultra in luxury"

The carrying capacity of the world is in jeopardy—governments around the world realize that something must be done to save the water and air supplies—they look to the automobile industry for help

Ford begins talking to Sony about merger; both realize they need an airline partner to reach the full potential for PTVs

2017   Ford-Sony-Boeing merge to create the FSB group

2018   FSB Group scraps all plans for vehicles with wheels and opts to spend all R&D money on PTVs

Companies begin to create a spaceway infrastructure of electro-magnetic fields for PTVs

2020   GM, VW, Nissan, Mercedes-Benz, Mitsubishi, Saab and Volvo are victims of information warfare

IBM absorbs GM and its "partners"

Electronics manufacturing in space begins

China emerges as the major economic power, followed by India (2), the EC (3), the U.S. (4), and Japan (5). Japan is the electronics capital of the world; India is the software capital.

2021   Money the world over is replaced by electronic "system dollars."

Currencies no longer exist.

2022   Intel buys Honda/Chrysler/BMW organization

World famine crises averted

2025   The spaceway infrastructure is completed

The education of two billion people via Microsoft Satellite System and the Big 10 changes the consciousness of the world

2028   Biosphere dome is built on Luna

2039   Biosphere dome on Mars is built

2040   "Driving" is outlawed everywhere in the system

2045   Construction of Earth's satellite cities begins

       Population of Earth is at the same level as 2000

2085   Organized crime syndicates create global alliances and become major shareholders of legitimate business; PTV companies must respond

       PTVs are drivable on Asimov for recreational purposes

Chapter 3

The Short Visioning Process Exercise

Frequently, it is not practical for an organization to invest the time and resources to develop a full 360 degree scenario for themselves, as long as a full scenario has been developed somewhere. When that happens, organizations can use the short process to approximate the larger version so that some benefits can be gained. This Chapter describes that process, as illustrated in Figure 3.1.

Figure 3.1   Macro Visioning Process Flow Diagram

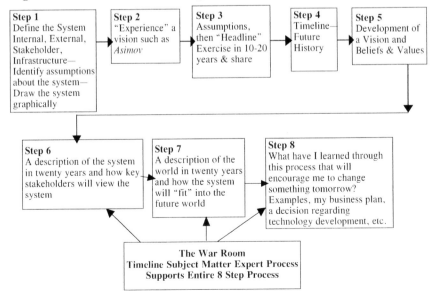

Step 1. Define the System

The short process begins with each individual in the planning team stating their top three assumptions about the current "system." The system is usually defined as that organization or sub-organization for which the process is being developed. The current "system" is then defined in its entirety. This includes the external environment, the internal environment, and the stakeholder environment as described in Figure 1 in Chapter 1. It is essential that the definition captures the identity of the system as it currently exists, not how it could be in the future.

External Environment

The external environment consists of those conditions in which the system operates. It includes the major political, military, governmental, economic, sociological, cultural, religious, technological and competitive forces in the world.

The more effectively an organization understands these forces the more likely they can anticipate the changes that will affect them. The identification and elaboration of these elements constitutes an effective external environmental scan. A scan is a process to identify important elements of the world or the organization and learn about them.

Stakeholder Environment

The stakeholder environment includes those individuals or groups who have a stake in the organization. The most important stakeholder for a business is the customer. Equally important is the employee. Without either stakeholder, there is no company. Regardless of the organization, there are customers who can be identified. They represent the users of the output from the organization, inside or outside. For example, in a consumer business, the buying public is the customer. Inside a manufacturing environment, there are multiple customers. They can range from the next person who receives the output of a process, to a dealer network that receives a product for distribution to the ultimate buyer of the product.

Other major stakeholders of organizations include suppliers, communities which benefit from the organization and its work, governments which are affected by or must regulate the organization, unions which represent a workforce, competitors who are affected by the organization, and other strategic "partners." A major stakeholder in most corporations include stockholders and the financial, investment communities. In government organizations, the stakeholders will include elected officials, such as Congress and The White House as well as the People of the United States in this country, on whose behalf they are working.

The more global an organization is, the more complex its stakeholder environment. Governments around the world become stakeholders, and their laws and regulations are essential to understand. It is one of the areas of overlap between the stakeholder and external environments. Every organization needs to understand its stakeholders and at any given point in time, how to communicate effectively with them.

Internal Environment

It is also important to regularly explore the internal environment of the organization. This includes the people of the organization and how well they work together, as a team, to accomplish the work of the organization. Is the organization structured effectively and efficiently to accomplish work or is the structure a barrier? What are the functions of the organization? How well do they work together? What is the organization's overall process capability? Is it measurable? What about process integration, that is, how does the process of one function interface with the process of another?

A crucial element of the internal environment is the culture of the organization. How would it be characterized? Is it a positive force for change in the organization or a barrier to change? Are there formal, written statements of beliefs and values? What does the company stand for?

How are decisions made? What is the resource allocation process? How does the organization invest in its leadership for future generations? What is the infrastructure which supports the entire organization? What are the organization's unique core competencies that separate it from others?

Identification of all these elements and the answering of all these questions, constitutes the internal environmental scan. In addition, it is typical for an organization to regularly ask its employees a variety of confidential questions to ensure regular feedback.

The System Draw

After the environments have been scanned, and the elements have been identified, it is useful to graphically draw the overall system and how the elements relate to one another. This is helpful, especially at the macro level.

The environmental scans and the system draw constitute defining the system.

Step 2. Experience a Vision

The next step in the Visioning Process is the presentation of an example of a vision. Ordinarily, this can be in written form to acquaint those developing the vision, or it can be described in oral form with or without visuals. What is most important is that those individuals who are developing a vision understand how comprehensive one can be. It frequently is helpful to go far into the future, like *Asimov*, to describe the vision. This enables the individuals to break out of their thought patterns, think "out of the box" and accept non-traditional ideas.

Step 3. The Headline Exercise

After experiencing the example, individuals are then asked to write a story in a year about twenty years into the future. Examples of headlines referring to their organization are provided, and they can write the story behind the headline, or they can make up their own headline in that time frame and write that story. This enables the individuals to create a future in their own minds. It also is a simple way to help people think creatively. This activity works well when people are grouped into two's or three's.

Individuals then share their stories with one another.

Step 4. Timeline Exercise

After the Headline exercise is completed, groups are asked to put together a timeline from the present out to twenty years or so, and asked to choose two or three areas that they will explore into the future along a timeline. The groups try to think through how an area might evolve over the time period, and what assumptions could occur year by year, though usually, groups think through the areas in 5 year intervals. This helps the groups think through plausible ways a future might unfold.

The timelines are then shared with the groups.

Step 5. Development of a Vision, Beliefs and Values

The groups are then asked to develop a set of assumptions that they have made about the year, twenty years out. These assumptions are then used by the groups to develop a vision statement. Normally, the facilitator develops a "straw-man" statement which the groups then try to use as a starting point, and several versions are developed until a consensus is developed. A statement of beliefs and values are also usually developed.

Step 6. Description of the System in 20 Years

A description of what the system will look like in twenty years is now developed, and how key stakeholders will view the organization in twenty years, ideally.

Step 7. Description of the World in 20 Years

A description of the state of the world in twenty years and how the "system" fits into the future world is then developed. Usually vision statements are descriptions of what an organizations *wants* to look like in twenty years; an ideal state.

Step 8. What Have I learned?

The visioning process is not meant to be a prediction or a forecast, but a learning process for those engaged in it, to more effectively focus the organization and point it in the right direction in a proactive way. Decision makers should ask themselves, "What have I learned through this process that will encourage me to change something tomorrow? Examples include business plans, technology plans, etc.

Note that Step 2 cannot be accomplished unless a full scenario was developed.

What follows is an example of the short visioning process, the UAW-GM example.

United Auto Workers—General Motors:
An Example

In the nineties, I had the privilege of working on visioning projects for two enormous institutions simultaneously; General Motors and the U.S. Department of Defense. In the process, I began to think about the national security community and what the vision of the country might be. It also became obvious to me that national security was economic security and that concept changed the way in which I would work with both organizations for years. In fact, I think my work with GM influenced my work with DoD and vice versa; the projects were actually "co-evolving."

General Motors in the late eighties and early nineties was in serious trouble, not too different from today. Although it has made enormous strides in the quality of its products and its global competitiveness, back then, the quality of their products was not nearly what it is today and the learning curve GM has been on for the last two decades that has begun to bridge the gap with the Japanese had barely begun. In the 1989 to 1996 timeframe, I had the opportunity to work with two visionary GM executives, Bob Dorn at Cadillac, and then, the Portfolio Engineering organization, and Vince Barabba, the head of marketing and corporate strategy. Later, I would have the privilege of working with Jay Wilber and Tom Walsh of the UAW-GM Quality Network, the union-management partnership at GM that defines and carries out the quality process.

My earliest work at GM was with Keith Cooley, the Staff Manager in the Engineering organization in December, 1988 who had approached me to help him with the Allanté program, an ultra-luxury convertible whose body was made by Pininfarina in Torino, Italy, flown to the U.S. and then finished at the Cadillac Detroit Hamtramck plant. The car had many problems, both in the quality arena and in terms of the business case. Keith and his team and I worked on those problems, eventually fixing the car. But, it was working with Keith's boss, Bob Dorn, Cadillac's Chief Engineer, when the Cadillac organization was an integrated car company, that I began my personal transformation process in terms of understanding General Motors and visioning processes.

Bob Dorn was a legend in the auto business. Of course, I knew who he was when he happened to sit next to me at a Dr. Deming conference in Washington, D.C. in January of 1989. But, of course, he didn't know me. What he also didn't know was that I was working with Keith Cooley and his team on the Allanté program. When we took a break, he was describing the positive things that were going on at Cadillac and I told him a few of my "observations." The look on his face said "Who are you and how do you know all this?" But, he just listened patiently. Over the next seven years, Bob and I would work together on many different projects at GM and he would inspire me to do some of the best work I have ever done in my life. This was especially true in our work with Dr. Deming on strategic and systemic thinking and bringing that to Cadillac.

For three years, from 1994-1996, I became a "captive" supplier to GM working on dozens of different projects with many different people. One project was to look ahead at the future of the company and write a visioning "thought and discussion piece" for Vince Barabba. Much of my work over the years with GM was this kind of special project. Another project output was with the UAW-GM Quality Network looking at the future of the relationship with Jay Wilber and Tom Walsh. The Quality Network project described in this chapter was not from my captive years since most of those projects are still too confidential to share. This project, in 1998, was undertaken after *Asimov* was written and is based on it using the short visioning process. There is simply no substitute for looking at an organization's visioning work to understand its power to teach and free up creative energy.

UAW-GM Quality Network

This project, for General Motors, was with the United Auto Workers—General Motors Quality Network (UAW-GM QN) leadership to explore alternative futures. This resulted in an interesting look at what the relationship between GM and its union partnership might evolve into. This was after *Asimov* had been developed, and we were able to piggy-back on the work. In 1998 GM was embroiled in a bitter struggle with its union partners that led to a strike. This effort began before the strike and continued after it. The visionary people who lead this effort, especially Jay Wilber and Tom Walsh who co-managed the Quality Network for GM management and the UAW, were able to step out into the next larger system, and for the good of the system, pull together a joint vision of the future, together. In retrospect, as I examine the outstanding progress that GM has made in the quality arena and the relationship between the UAW and GM management, the reality of this work and its hopes for the future, are becoming reality.

What follows is an excerpt of the results of that effort and an example of the short visioning process output.

UAW-GM QUALITY NETWORK

In the spring of 1998, the UAW-GM Quality Network leadership, both union and management, decided to use the visioning process in a joint environment. This report documents the entire process and the results.

The process requires a definition of "the system" for which the vision would be developed. The "UAW-GM Relationship" was the defined system.

Assumptions About the Current System

The following were identified as assumptions about the current system.

- The inertia of the status-quo inhibits our ability to see much beyond today in our relationships.
- The relationship is one to be reacted to; not proactively planned to support mutual goals.
- There is no shared vision of the future of opportunities for cooperation domestically or around the world.

The Complexity of the Issues Which Emerged from the Process

The following issues were identified during the process:

- Wall Street expects reduced structural costs, but understands little about what it would take to "grow the business."
- The union workforce accounts for less than 10% of total cost, yet seems to be the focus of most cost reduction; what about the other 90%?
- "Core competencies" are not understood by senior management because they are difficult to put a value on—like knowledge.

"Hoped For" Assumptions About the System in the Year 2020

The following were identified as the assumptions the team would hope for in the year 2020:

- Both GM and the UAW will be strong, viable organizations.
- The National and local agreements will be living agreements.
- The UAW holds a seat on the GM Board of Directors.
- The Labor Relations function has disappeared and has been replaced by a people-focused process; HRD is a joint activity.
- The focus will be sincerely on growing the business—both parties will work together and mutually benefit; trust and mutual respect of all are the way we manage the business.
- GM's *global* workforce can buy the product it builds.
- GM is the employer of choice in all areas worldwide.
- GM products and services are in demand.
- GM has 30% of the global market share.

Conclusions and Recommendations for Future Actions

- There is a great deal of common ground between the UAW and GM management in that both want an improved relationship; both believe the current relationship is *not* conducive to win-win.
- The trial team believes that the process is worthwhile to engage people in discussions of the real issues within a structured process; the current environment does not permit a sufficient amount of on-going discussion.
- Only the senior-most leadership can reaffirm the Quality Network Beliefs and Values, and perhaps, should sign their names to another document like The Toledo Accord. (the original statement of beliefs and values)
- The General Motors University should be able to play a role in "jointness" education and training; curriculum for the Quality College could be developed to include the philosophy of Dr. Deming and the many statistical tools available are taught routinely.
- The GMU may also need to teach "joint" systems and strategic thinking and how this perspective can improve the long-term viability of the company and its ultimate global competitiveness and success.
- The UAW-GM Leadership Quality Council should develop a *joint vision* for the 21st century with this process to ensure a stronger General Motors and its relationship to the UAW

in the next century, but GM's top management must personally lead the effort.

For the purposes of this process, the system was defined as the "UAW-GM relationship." One individual characterized the aim of this system as, "A relationship that facilitates the achievement of the goals of each party."

To begin the process, the teams were asked to describe the three main assumptions that they held about the current system. Then, they were asked to "draw" their system as it currently exists, as a preparation to think about the system as they know it. The external forces, internal elements and stakeholders of the system were identified by each group.

The next step in the process consisted of showing the teams what a future vision might look like. I presented a "vision" slide show which portrayed the Asimov scenario. It showed one potential future which could occur, and how General Motors and the UAW, the institutions in the system, might evolve.

With the mindset of the future scenario, the individuals were asked to think about the assumptions they might make coming back to the year 2020, and the teams identified some of those assumptions. Individuals were asked to think about other assumptions they might make, and to bring those assumptions to the next session.

Individuals did much of their work in teams of three or four. At the beginning of session two, the teams were asked to describe the assumptions that they *would like to be true* about the system in the year 2020, and those assumptions were shared.

Next, the teams were asked to write a headline and article for a "virtual magazine" that would describe their system in 2020. Examples of headlines were provided. The groups wrote their stories and shared those stories with everyone.

Finally, each group was asked to develop a timeline of events, from today to the year 2020 that could lead to one of their hoped for assumptions coming true. This process, which took the most time to develop, produced a plausible scenario of events. Those time-lines were also shared.

In session three, areas of common ground were communicated based on the work in session two, and led to much discussion of issues. The teams were then asked to describe their "ideal system" or the ideal UAW-GM relationship in the year 2020. Those were shared with the entire group. And, finally, the groups were asked to develop a vision statement. There were two groups in session three, and two vision statements emerged.

What follows is a synthesis of the work of all three sessions.

Initial Assumptions About the Current System

- UAW-GM leadership believes that high quality and low cost products and services are essential to the viability of GM, but haven't come to an agreement on the process to get there.
- Top leadership must develop a credible and trusting relationship through their actions and must never compromise. Managers must drive the process.
- There are areas of common interest that are shared between the UAW and GM, such as the quality of our products, the health and safety of our people, education and training, leadership behavior, volunteerism, etc. These need to be jointly planned, developed, lead and managed.
- There are areas where the UAW and GM disagree, such as the methods to remain competitive, methods for reducing cost, methods for increasing revenue, and jobs.
- The view of the relationship from the outside by the public, the customer and the press could be improved if we could genuinely work jointly and not air our differences in the press through frustration.
- The majority of people in both parties want to improve the relationship.
- GM and the UAW have a symbiotic relationship; that is, one cannot survive without the other.
- If there is an answer to improving the relationship on a long term basis, communication will play an important role.

Definition of System

Although the richness of the system maps would be impossible to reproduce, the major elements of the system; external forces, internal issues and processes and stakeholders have been captured.

Stakeholders of the System

The following stakeholders were identified:

- Customers
- Employees
- Suppliers
- Stockholders
- Communities
- Governments
- Competitors
- Unions
- General Motors management
- Families
- Consultants
- Media
- Dealers
- Environment
- Money lenders/financial community/Wall Street
- Retirees

External, Societal Forces

The following external forces and influences were identified:

- World politics
- Global economy and monetary policy
- Competitors' relations with unions
- Educational systems
- Society's perception of unions and industry
- Global fads
- Interest rates
- Environment
- Technology trends
- Domestic politics
- Wall Street analysts
- Government regulators—US and others
- External measurements, such as Harbour, JD Power, *Consumer Reports, etc.*

External Issues to Relationship, but Internal to GM and UAW

The following elements are more complex. They are not external societal forces, but may be external to the relationship, and depending on your point of view, can be internal to the relationship.

- UAW business beyond GM, such as with Delphi
- GM global thrust
- Basic philosophy of GM and UAW
- Product plan/portfolio
- Divestiture policy
- UAW and GM Management progression/succession
- Leadership turnover at both organizations
- Age of the workforce—difficult to change
- Speed of technology; technology paradigm

Internal Issues and Processes to UAW-GM Relationship

- Quality Network
- Local contracts
- National agreements
- Beliefs and values
- Compensation policy
- Labor relations
- Leadership communications
- Volunteerism
- Personal relationships
- Leadership turnover
- Technology paradigms
- Health and safety
- Integrity issues
- Long range potential and strength of the product
- Level of dialog between management and union
- Level of innovation

At the Hourly and Salaried Employee Level the employee should be:

- Trusted
- Trained
- Aware
- Respected
- Involved
- Financially secure
- Recognized for contributions
- Empowered
- Well equipped
- Knowledgeable

Assumptions about the year 2020 . . .

Before leaving after day one, the participants were asked to think about the ideas of the vision work to date, and prepare their assumptions about the year 2020. When they arrived at day two, several individuals presented their ideas, which follow:

- Medical technology will clone everything
- We will environmentally clean-up the ozone breech prior to polar melt
- More and more wealth will be shifted to an ever increasing elite class
- The United States will shrink in influence as other centers of untapped natural resources emerge as ours become depleted
- More public transportation will be used rather than personal vehicles
- The information age will truly emerge as computers become a natural part of everyone's lives
- Alternative energy sources will have to be developed as natural oil and gas is used up
- Health care will advance causing much longer and healthier lives for the general population with the rich and elite enjoying extreme advances in health care and regeneration
- 20% of automobiles and trucks will be powered by other than internal combustion engines

- The average cost of an automobile will be $65,000
- Standard on all new cars and trucks will be: cellular phones, televisions, computers, navigation systems, two-way visual communication
- Several electrical functions will be voice activated
- Public transportation will increase significantly in all metro areas
- Telephone cords will be a thing of the past
- Cellular phones will be standard features on all cars and trucks
- OnStar type systems will be standard with expanded features (e.g. diagnostics)
- The life span of the vehicle skin will be 30 years and will be made of a material that has yet to be discovered
- Pagers as we know them will no longer exist; it will be a sophisticated combination of cellular phone, computer, and pager, with visual display
- Gene therapy will eliminate 80% of known cancers
- Average hospital stays will be less than two days
- 90% of surgeries will be done on an outpatient basis
- Consumption of red meat will be reduced by 30%
- Fruit and vegetable consumption will be increased by 50%
- Only 10% of typical bills will be paid by writing a check
- The average UAW base hourly wage rate will be $42.00 per hr.
- 80% of salaried employees in the auto industry will be contract employees
- Life expectancy will be 92 for women and 89 for men
- Social security will be replaced by privately administered and self funded retirement
- 50% of components for cars will be made outside of U.S. or Canada
- The cost of a college education will be $175,000 for private schools and $100,000 for state schools
- 50% of line workers will have at least an associates degree
- 30% of all retail purchases will be made by computer
- There will be an average of two computers in every home
- Hand held computers with the capabilities greater than current desktops will be used by 50% of the working population

- There will still be cars and trucks on roads, but they will be nearly 95%+ recycled by the OEM's who now see their business as supplying transportation for their customers for their life
- Vehicles operate on main roads of transportation using computer driven entry, exit and operation to maximize the flow, and improve the vehicle safety since the cost of accidents, insurance and loss of life and injury can no longer be tolerated in a world where compounding knowledge dictates a life long investment in people
- Congestion in inner cities has been solved since grid-lock is no longer tolerated by the people who work there
- The third world will have learned methods to conserve natural resources from North America and will use conservation strategies that have been adopted by all the countries of the world
- Recycling has been the responsibility of manufacturers for 10 years, and products have been developed since the late 1990s that were designed with materials that were re-used to create new products
- Recycling methods are being used to re-manufacture componentry that will be used to keep the transportation fleet current by law for safety, communications and emissions/ fuel economies
- Many people work at home to help improve congestion and emissions from vehicles—they have become even more productive in many ways since they no longer need to move to their place of work
- Students at universities may take courses from any other university in the world through distance learning methods
- Communications systems are all wireless
- There will be a world wide currency on one system
- There will be factories in space
- Man will have been to Mars
- Most products, product packaging and shipping containers are recyclable or biodegradable
- Energy is widely available and relatively inexpensive except for petroleum-based fuels which are expensive and highly taxed

- Preventive medicine is the norm from pre-natal care to death and an annual check-up prescribes any medication necessary to maintain a healthful state
- Most medical treatment is for injury rather than disease
- While individual countries still exist, the world is divided into six de facto economic regions, each dominated by a local super-power

Assumptions About the Year 2020 We Want to See

After looking at the assumptions which people brought to the session, the groups were asked to develop a list of system assumptions that they would like to see in the year 2020. The system was defined as the "UAW-GM Relationship." Those assumptions are described below.

- The UAW and GM will be strong, viable organizations
- The National and local (all) Agreements will be living agreements
- UAW holds a seat on the GM Board
- GM global workforce can afford to buy the products it builds
- GM global workforce has good, equitable health care
- 50% of GM vehicles do not have internal combustion engines
- There is diversified leadership in both organizations
- Labor-relations function has gone away; HRD is jointly managed, chairman of the shop committee is a member of the plant manager's staff, all joint activities people are jointly appointed on both sides, there are no more "old Joes" and "marginal Marys"
- Manufacturing runs the business—not finance
- Every employee, regardless of job function, is required to have 30 days of in-plant, off-line training and 30 days of on-line training
- The focus will sincerely be on growing the business—both parties will work together and mutually benefit
- GM is the employer of choice in all areas worldwide
- GM is the company of choice worldwide
- GM has 30% of the global market share
- There will be a global equivalent of the AFL/CIO and all unions will work with management to improve the global standard of living

- GM and its subsidiaries will dominate the 3 major global markets; the western hemisphere, Europe and Asia
- Over 50% of global vehicles have alternative fuel systems
- GM will survive joined to a major Japanese company whose leadership will take over to improve GM's capability with people, customers, society, suppliers, and other stakeholders
- The Board of Directors will be very much connected to the transformation of GM as a corporation that has and continues to make its rightful contribution to its customers, employees, society and other stakeholders

Headline Exercise

With the groups wish-lists of assumptions completed, each group was then asked to prepare a headline for a "virtual" newsletter for the Quality Network in the year 2020, and write the story behind the headline. *This gave the groups the opportunity to experience strategic futuring, first-hand.*

The following stories are examples of what was developed.

- **UAW-GM Unveils Its Plan To Pilot Its Alternative-Fuel Powered Public Transportation System in Metropolitan Detroit**

At ground-breaking ceremonies today, the UAW President, the City Mayor and the GM Chairperson revealed the blueprints of their new alternative-fuel powered public transportation system tying in Pontiac, Lansing, Flint, Toledo, Port Huron, Ann Arbor and Metro Airport.

Partnering with GM and the UAW are state, local, and federal governments, NASA and the U.S. Departments of Transportation and Energy. The project will provide an estimated 20,000 additional jobs to create and maintain the infrastructure and guidance systems.

As world leaders in environmental stewardship, GM and the UAW estimate this system will virtually eliminate greenhouse gases in the area.

"We see this as the culmination of twenty years of renaissance and revitalization efforts spearheaded by our partnership with the UAW," said the GM Chairperson.

"With the production processes and systems jointly developed by our membership and our GM partners, we have accelerated our original production timelines threefold and plan to offer regularly scheduled service in 18 months," the UAW President announced.

The City Mayor stated simply, "This should be a model for all urban areas."

- **World Peace Organization Commends Union-Management Partnership at GM**

The World Peace Organization (WPO) today commended the union-management partnership within General Motors for their joint contribution to the improvement of the global standard of living. The WPO, representing all nations, was formed following the cooperation of Greenpeace, the United Nations and the State of the World Forum.

Following General Motors acquisition of Honda, the company recognized the need to capture at least 30% of the Asian market. They, therefore, formed a joint venture called New China Motors, formerly known as the Chinese Government First Autoworks. Together, with Honda, General Motors exceeded its goal and currently has 33.5% of the Asian market comparable to its share in the other two major global markets.

Today, the WPO Chairperson discussed the history of GM's partnering with its union and people. She stated that following the consolidations of the UAW, CAW, IUE, USW and CTM from North America, the new global union, GTW (Global Transportation Workers) was formed and aligned with IG Metall. The GM Chairman, together with the President of the GTW decided that the only true job security comes through working together toward a common vision and a well-executed Total Quality System. Their shared vision included being certain all GM global employees could afford the products they built.

The impact of that vision has resulted in all stakeholders of the GM system benefiting from its success. Communities and suppliers, in particular, throughout the world have benefited from GM's growth. As a result, the standard of living has improved throughout the world from this single shared vision. A representative from the GTW, who started a foundational process in 1987, referred to as the Quality Network, received the award from WPO. He cited the Chairman of GM with having the vision and the leadership skills necessary to transform General Motors management style into a people focused company of choice. That philosophy, together with the shared vision made the difference, breaking a long standing adversarial relationship.

Time-Line Exercise

The final exercise of the day was the longest. The groups were asked to choose one or two assumptions that they want to have happen. Each group was then asked to write out a timeline, in 5 year intervals, of the events that would need to occur and when, in order to make their assumption(s) come true. Ultimately, timelines can lead to the development of a shared vision and a business plan to accomplish the vision.

Assumption: Global Unions are Working in Partnership with General Motors Management

2000

- Union management summit creates joint vision and commitment. Discussions were led by the GM and the UAW President
- All grievances and disciplines canceled. Partners start with clean sheet of paper.
- Parties draft a new "Toledo Accord" that reflects the joint commitment consistent with Beliefs and Values. Measurement system developed and implemented.
- All union and management meetings are open to joint participation.
- All employees are given a minimum of 100 hours of job/skill improvement training per year.
- Traditional Labor Relations is transformed to become a people focused leadership organization.
- GM acquires Honda. Honda's focus on people and the production system attracts GM and markets.
- GM management influenced by Honda's management style behaves as if there is no union and treats its employees with respect and provides consistent, honest and timely information.
- Union leadership responds to management focus on people in a positive way by electing new progressive leaders.
- Union local leaders' terms are extended for stability. Management and union leaders are nominated for positions by joint HRM Councils.

- The Delphi Manufacturing System, Competitive Manufacturing and Lean Engineering are consolidated into the Quality Network to form the General Motors Global Production System.

2005

- Global union emerges from UAW, IUE, CAW, USW, CTW and IG Metall consolidation.
- Global union-management leadership conducts summit meeting and drafts global joint objectives including management system. Both business and social objectives are included.
- Global suggestion plan becomes treasure trough for creativity and innovation.
- Global contract based on beliefs and values is negotiated with leadership of all unions simultaneously.
- Reward and recognition process based on objective criteria is applied to everyone. Pay is based on knowledge, skills, experience and contributions to meeting global objectives. All employees are on salary.
- GM suppliers have status as full partners with product life agreements. Most are unionized because the union has become an attractive manager and supplier of skilled workers.

2010

- Global contract becomes living agreement and is modified as required during annual global union-management summit meetings.
- A global union-management summit drafts a joint 10 year business plan with growth in market share and the improvement of employees' standards of living being complementary objectives based on the belief that all employees should be able to afford the product they build. The goal of 30% of the global vehicle market is established. The president of the Global Union is appointed to the GM Presidents Council.
- Union leaders are appointed to GM Strategic Planning Council.

2015

- Global union-management summit meets and evaluates progress. General Motors has 30% of the global market and 90% of all GM employees own GM vehicles that are not more than 2 years old.
- All employees are recognized by union-management leadership with special stock options and cash bonuses.
- All global manufacturing facilities are self-directed work teams with no direct supervision. Joint strategy boards set manufacturing operation objectives and goals.
- Employees are fully empowered to meet those objectives and goals. The self-directed work teams make all decisions. Unresolved issues are referred to the joint strategy board for resolution.

2020

- GM union-management leadership recognized by World Peace Organization for their contribution to improving the standard of living world-wide for GM employees as well as the positive impact they have had on communities and suppliers.
- GM union-management leadership is recognized as the global benchmark for partnership.
- GM has 33.5% of the global new vehicle market share. RONA is 15.5% with a 7% net margin. GM share price hits $300.
- GM voted "Best Global Company" by its employees and its customers.

Example of Vision State for the Year 2020

The vision of General Motors is to be recognized as the "best" corporation in the world by its stakeholders:

- GM has selected transportation products and services as their business
- GM is the employer of choice to work for
- GM treats their people and their suppliers as they treat their customers—with respect and courtesy

- GM is known as having the highest value products available that best serve the customers' needs and aspirations; they are the customers' products and services of choice
- GM is trusted by the communities in which they live and work; they are a contributing and active member of the community and add value to all aspects of community life
- The UAW is a value-adding member of the "enterprise" helping to make GM better as a result of the relationship to its stakeholders: employees, customers, communities, stockholders, suppliers
- The UAW is the union of choice
- The UAW is known for developing its people and employees, and its "state of the art" tools and processes to help achieve the most qualified work force in the world, who are highly recruited by others
- There are regular opportunities for dialogue between management and the union; there is a UAW member on the GM Board of Directors; Quality Councils are operating the system for which they are accountable to their operating plan
- The UAW are asked for their inputs to the training, selection, and discussions about future managers; in fact, this is a joint training process that includes UAW people who teach the new managers before they are put on the job
- Areas of mutual interest of the union and the management of GM continue to grow

Conclusion

There are many areas of common ground. The process of visioning can be used to develop a common vision of the future, and may be the single greatest way to leverage General Motors leadership in management and the union so they collectively can manage the company in the 21st century.

Areas of common ground already exist with Joint Leadership:

- "Partnering" is a value between GM and the UAW, as well as other stakeholders.
- Environmental stewardship is a value.
- Global competitiveness is a value.
- Customers, suppliers and employees are equal priorities.

- Technology will continue to drive change.
- Having employees who can afford to buy GM products around the world is a value, which will drive up the global standard of living.
- The only true job security will come through working together toward a common vision and a well-executed Total Quality System.
- Adversarial relationships are not useful.
- There is a need for a joint vision and commitment to the future.
- Win-win is a virtue; indeed, a united Win, with a capital W.
- There is a need to reconfirm the "Toledo Accord" that reflects the current joint commitment consistent with the Beliefs and Values and a new measurement system along with it.
- Traditional Labor Relations needs to be transformed into a people focused leadership organization.
- Management needs to behave as if there is no union and needs to treat its employees with respect and provide consistent, honest and timely information to all parties.
- Both business and social objectives need to be developed.
- The union has become an attractive manager and supplier of skilled workers.
- Global contract should become a living agreement and modified as required annually.
- Contentious union-management relations and work stoppages are a thing of the past.
- GM continues to grow marketshare world-wide.
- UAW membership is extended outside North America, especially in third world countries.
- All employees are on the same reward system.
- There is trust and respect of all parties.

Remembrances

The relationship between the UAW and GM has steadily improved since the time when they engaged in this project in 1998. Recently, one of GM's plants in the United States had among the highest customer satisfaction ratings ever, their safety record has become the standard of the world, and their ability to compete with the best in the world in product is coming to pass. None of that could have happened without a strong relationship between union and management.

In the last decade, General Motors has also come to understand that it is a system and it continues to invest in learning and knowledge. The company is always in "search and learn" mode. This is the best way I know of for a company to succeed in the long run.

Chapter 4

The Tartan Scenario: Visions of a Consumer Company—Tartan Transport & Technologies, Ltd. In the Year 2010

Introduction

The Tartan scenario was developed as a thought-provoking exercise to help think through competitive intelligence issues with regard to a potential competitor for Ford Motor Company. It used elements of both visioning processes and might be described as a hybrid process. As with all scenarios, the story is fictitious and was used for instructional purposes only.

While developing this scenario, The University Group explored several aspects of running a business.

Diversity: What impact did racial, cultural, religious and gender diversity have on the development of the company? How are these differences celebrated?

Intellectual Assets (IA): Do intellectual assets manifest themselves in more than one way? Is it possible that brand is an intellectual asset? Is the customer relationship an IA? What develops the relationship with a customer for life? Is it knowledge? How do we evaluate an asset that is not static and difficult to measure?

Global Community: How is a true global community defined? We broadly defined it to include every element of society, including government, academia and industry. How is it used to develop a real and basic relationship? What are the implications of a global community to the company and the customer? Is it possible to give back more than you take as an obligation to next generations—while still making a profit?

Systemic Understanding: How can a company better understand the interdependence of one industry with another? Does the company understand where it fits in the future vis-a-vis the competitors? Does the company understand the relationship to all elements of industry, such as utilities, education, health services, communications and banking? How would partnerships between industry, government and academia impact the scenario?

History

As the Tartan family looks back over the last ten years, it is clear that the decisions made then, to broaden the scope of the enterprise, are working well. The strategy that was implemented at that time included the development of comprehensive infrastructure process capability in three large-scale areas; the global movement of people, goods and services, information and money for 1) personal use, 2) commercial and governmental use, and 3) military use.

Because today's vision of the Tartan family is the essence of "mobility" around the globe, the company has become one of the few organizations that has survived its origins from the industrial society and become a leader in the information society of the twenty-first century.

At one time, Tartan thought that its future was only in the car and truck transportation businesses, although it also owned diverse businesses such as financial services, information and telecommunications services and military services. With the inculcation of continuous learning as a value and with the strategic management of both the human and business sides of the enterprise, Tartan was able to see beyond its core business to what it would take to establish itself as a global leader in a twenty-first century of "virtual" organizations. Indeed, had Tartan chosen the path of staying in its narrowly defined car and truck businesses, it would not have survived a future which included competitors who all adapted.

Tartan was able to see that the global opportunities of the early part of the twenty-first century would be vastly different from the ones they then experienced because the business paradigm would be different. The paradigm of the twentieth century was founded upon analysis, and the mechanistic breaking apart into component pieces of an entity to understand the whole. Tartan was able to anticipate what we now know today; that the paradigm of the twenty-first century is the strategic, holistic understanding of synergies and synthesis in order to create a whole, whose value-chain is more than the sum of its parts.

The ideas of a Tartan virtual family were not new. From the days of its founder, the company was convinced its most important assets were the people in its major stakeholder "family;" its customers, its suppliers, its dealers, its employees. So it is not surprising that almost ten years ago, Tartan was able to see and take advantage of the virtual paradigm which transformed the entire industrial and information infrastructure of the world.

At that time, Tartan saw its future world as one which would defeat the idea of the "Zero Sum Game," an archaic notion that the world must have winners at the expense of losers. Today, of course, it is clear that all must be able to win in order to have a prosperous and peaceful world. At the end of the last century, it was not uncommon for countries to mobilize their resources to economically defeat other nations even at a time when those nations were essential for long term survival. It was not uncommon to destroy the environment at the expense of all for the sake of a few corporate profits. It was not uncommon for companies to take advantage of the organizations and stakeholders that it required for survival, instead of bringing them in as partners in their business. Indeed, the notion that being good global citizens was the secret to good global business was not always understood.

Tartan Today

Tartan is one of the world's leading corporations, today. Many look to Tartan for leadership, whose client base now includes individuals from every country in the world, most countries of the world, and most of the world's military establishments.

Tartan has taken the notion of systems integration and strategic management and has married them in a global way to meet the needs of its many customers across the board and around the world. Their work is one of merging and synthesizing diverse activities into value-added chains that produce far more than the sum of their parts. Tartan has taken a myriad of organizations and stakeholders and pulled them together in boundary-less, but stable relationships that provide the fundamental infrastructures that define the world of today; infrastructures which make up the very fabric of the lives of individuals, their organizations, and their countries.

What follows are a few examples of products and services that are available through Tartan's various infrastructures.

Personal Infrastructure
Process Capability in 2010

For the individual and family in society today, Tartan's personal and household infrastructure process capability can best be illustrated by describing a few examples of products and services developed for these global customers.

Tartan is in the car, van and light truck market providing personal transportation to individuals around the globe and into space. The vehicle systems today are also filled with telecommunications capabilities that enable the vehicle to be a full service communications center for office or home. Vehicles today include voice-activated telephones, computers, television, audio and video systems, and teleconferencing.

Vehicles have, as standard, on-board navigation systems that increase safety and efficiency as standard for years. When another vehicle comes too close, the warning systems automatically take steps to avoid a collision and warn the driver using voiced instructions. All vehicles, today, have an interval maintenance function that can lock on to the vehicle in front of it maintaining distance and speed and permitting the driver in the front vehicle to drive while the driver in the rear vehicle can rest. Most roads in large cities communicate to vehicles warning of potential slowdowns, hazards along the way and potential weather conditions. Tartan's acquisition of Mitsubishi Electronics enabled the company to improve its electronics capabilities immensely.

If the vehicle is broken into, its internal electronics automatically shut down its starting capability and send a message to the police who can trace the vehicle if someone is successful in moving it.

Tartan vehicles are known for their special DNA embedded in each of the components of the vehicle. These electronic "keys" enable, through electronic communications knowledge of where the vehicle is at any time, if something is wrong with the vehicle or if the vehicle breaks down for any reason. The DNA automatically sends a road repair vehicle and lets the driver know how long they must wait. At the same time, members of the family are notified so they can be in contact with the vehicle as it waits.

The new space-station is nearing completion and needs fifty new vehicles. Tartan has won the contract because of its satellite capability in both global and off world areas.

Commercial and/or Governmental Infrastructure Capability

For the organization in society (company or country), Tartan's infrastructure capabilities are as powerful as they are in the personal arena. Some examples of this infrastructure follow.

Tartan manufactures light and heavy-duty trucks that utilize systems to insure the most efficient and effective delivery in the world. These vehicles also enable the loading and unloading of goods that are tracked electronically on a global basis using the Tartan satellite and navigation systems capability.

Goods are also tracked whether they are sent on planes, on Tartan powered trains along with other vehicles, or on the shuttles to the space-station. Tartan's satellites carry the major traffic of information and fund activity.

The manufacturing processes today require the integration of all segments of an organization and the design and engineering of products that utilize systems that automatically integrate and dynamically simulate. These enable suppliers and other stakeholders of systems to communicate with and function as a part of a seamless system regardless of where they are located or when they perform their services, and enable funds transfer on a real time basis increasing the cost efficiency of the system.

Tartan's satellites are also available for other services to organizations such as assisting in the forecasting of global weather, oil and mineral prospecting, and monitoring of the environment.

Military Infrastructure Capability

For the military in society today, Tartan's infrastructure is very helpful. The role of the military has changed considerably over the last ten years. Today, military establishments are far more oriented toward maintaining peace than waging wars. The skirmishes that escalated into major wars only a few years ago are no longer permitted to get out of hand. Using

Tartan's command, control, communications, computers, intelligence and information (C^4I^2) satellites and systems, originally developed for NATO, a continuous monitoring of political "hot-spots" enables the military to watch out for trouble and intervene before major aggression can go very far.

In the event it must be prepared to wage a hot war or take aggressive action, Tartan's systems permit the military to be in control using the latest technologies.

These systems enable the Commander in Chief to talk with the soldier in the trenches if that is, indeed, what is needed. In addition, the powerful intelligence mechanisms set-up to collect, analyze, interpret and synthesize the enormous quantities of data available, give today's commanders the information they need when they need it. But, it is the interactive capabilities of the Tartan systems that provide the greatest power. Today's commander can "see" the action on television, can communicate with a soldier or give orders instantaneously in an encrypted message that only his soldiers can understand, and monitor in an interactive way. Soldiers can ask for help, or, without leaving the comfort and safety of their facilities, computerized "smart" weapons can find the enemy or its strategic strongholds and destroy them based on Tartan technologies.

In fact, today, Tartan satellites can take pictures of extraordinary resolution over just about any target area, or eavesdrop on communications, or intercept telemetry (the signals used to track and monitor the status of missiles). These tools augment traditional tools such as laser radar and other sensors.

Tartan's satellite systems also ensure that, even if land based communications systems are destroyed, communications will not be disrupted because all communications can go directly through the satellite systems.

Tartan's systems can also shape the data in ways that allow them to compare the actual state of natural conditions and enemy and friendly forces with the desired state. These systems can also give the commander fast access to relevant maps, environmental details, and expert advice—anything from a data bank of principles, doctrine, military history, and political objectives for synthesis.

Even though the world has become a safer place in the last ten years, nuclear weapons are still readily available, and so the need to keep the peace is essential. Also essential is the Tartan technology that permits the detection and elimination of a nuclear missile *before* any damage can be done, thus ensuring that peace is kept. Even the global positioning system satellites carry nuclear detection system packages. And, now that the military services around the globe all communicate with one another using common systems developed by Tartan, the ability to keep the peace is ever greater.

Today, as the military infrastructure examines its role in the new global-space system, it will carry with it the Tartan capability to keep the peace on earth and beyond.

2010 Scenario Descriptions for Toyota Tartan Transport Technologies (T4)

System Profile

Toyota Tartan Transport Technologies (T4) in 2010 is a global transport corporation which has its dominant presence for both manufacturing and market share, in Europe, Asia and North America. It is a joint venture between Toyota Motor Company of Toyota City, Japan and Tartan Transport Technologies Limited of Toronto, Canada.

The T4 president is Theodore Upson Tartan III (Trey), who is the genius behind the Transformer vehicle, which comprises the product line of T4. Although detractors feel that T3 should have kept complete ownership and control of the Transformer, industry analysts believe that the T4 partnership provides each party with strong benefits, which should lead to both profits and learning. More than a strategic alliance, T4 was structured through a 10% stock swap of the two companies.

Toyota Tartan Transport Technologies (T4) is viewed as the "new relationship" model of the industrial experience. T4 has the challenge and the honor of being the first true east-west equal partnership. It is the intent of the two parties to pursue perfect assimilation of the best of both companies, in terms of systems and culture. (Note: A seamless assimilation transcended the more traditional concept of integration, where lines still remain visible.)

A multitude of companies, including all of the automotive manufacturers, have tried various types of alliances and purchases, to gain market share, profits, and knowledge. The T4 alliance is viewed as unique in terms of the equality of its structure—albeit non-traditional. Both companies believe that both their intangible assets are more valuable to the venture than their tangible assets, and both see parity of what they will give with what they will get.

System Description

Vision: Personal Transport—Today and Tomorrow

"T4 is committed to touching the lives of the seven billion consumers in T4's community through personal mobility relationships."

Mission:
- To set all standards for relationships in personal, affordable, flexible and durable transport for the earth's community.

Values:
1. Strengthen relationships through continuous learning
2. Celebrate the individual differences of a truly diverse work force
3. Sustain the world community for generations
4. Be better tomorrow than today

Objectives:

Attain or exceed:
- Return on Customer Relationships (ROCR) of 95%
- Return on Investment (ROI) of 15%
- Return on Employee Contentment (ROEC) of 70%
- Return on Community Investment (ROCI) of 25%

Stakeholder Environment

Governments

Governmental scanning helps T4 to work with countries to plan investment, to address societal needs and anticipate demand. Scanning also forewarns T4 of potential issues and political problems that may impact their marketing and manufacturing efforts.

T4's relationship with the national governments is expected to be even stronger than either T3's or Toyota's. This is in part because of the extraordinary impact that T3 has made through its community investment programs. Although no company can enter a market without careful review of its Return on Community Investment (ROCI) metrics history, it is believed that the coordination of Toyota and Tartan efforts will yield even greater improvements.

Given T4's global presence, governments become a major stakeholder in the Joint Venture. T4's decision to establish a European headquarters in Brussels was hailed as an innovative approach to efficient
interaction with the varied and complex nature of European politics and
EEC regulation.

Competitors

The T4 venture will expand both partners' learning about competition.
Both partners currently have competing products and services. Both partners are aware of their own strengths and weaknesses relative to one
another, as well as to other competitors.

Because T4 recognizes that its understanding of consumers at a physical, emotional and experiential level is the very fiber of the comprehensive relationships they are building, they must identify and attract employees whose expertise is in industries that understand the consumer in
multiple ways. Therefore, T4 actively scans industries like health care,
entertainment, religion, and communications to identify the Intellectual
Assets that the business needs to stay competitive.

Because they owned the network, AT&T also had access to the data.
Over time, they learned to synthesize data into knowledge. With their
network roots, AT&T has become a consummate learner, severely challenging T4's learning competency.

Customers/Consumers

There are few differences between a customer and a consumer at T4.
The needs of both are of equal importance to R&D. The big difference is
the level of cooperation, and therefore personal contentment information
captured by T4. There is significant personal information captured on
customers as well, particularly through *luvtartan.com*. This information,
however, is not disaggregated from the whole until the consumer con-
verts to a customer.

At luvtartan.com, consumers can learn, not only about vehicles and
services, but how Tartan improves their lives and communities. Continuously updated, visitors to the "world love" site are informed of technical advances, new partnerships, research and products. Tartan com-
municates how, by being in business, it is contributing to improvements
in economic prosperity, social responsibility and community issues. There
is a cyber-mentoring service which, somewhat like the Peace Corps,

matches communities and companies in need with experts who can lend assistance.

The electronic impulse connection with the customers correlates with their subliminal needs (more under Core Competencies). This critical input, received through luvtartan.com, is a large factor in the calculation of Return on Customer Relationship (ROCR).

There are many other stakeholders that are investigated during the Stakeholder Scanning process. These include suppliers, stockholders, employees and communities.

External Environment

Political/Military

T4 has a political scanning process, which is defined in terms of physical presence, market potential and capital and human investment. Each is scanned continuously, but at different levels of detail. There is also a process for conducting regular scanning for countries which have been identified as potentially strategically important in the future.

Sociological/Culture/Religious

Tartan views the system as a single group of interrelated actions—Tartan's system cannot be separated from the global community. Consequently, Tartan has a responsibility both to improve the community and the company. As such, Tartan has developed a system which monitored 22 base social trends on an annual basis for nearly two decades. This information ranged from the standard demographic (population growth rates) to the more unusual (number of employees who speak more than 4 languages).

Once T4 was formed, both Tartan and Toyota had to create a new process, one which integrated cultural perceptions as to the importance and implications of those trends on both the system and the "*market of one.*" The "market of one" reminds every employee at T4 that every consumer on the planet is unique, their needs are valid, and their perspective is valuable.

Technological and Knowledge Building

Technological scanning is a complex T4 scanning process. Every stakeholder in the company is a part of this scanning process. Inputs come from Intellectual Property (knowledge and patent search), marketing (competitive assessments and relationship studies), manufacturing, academia and suppliers.

A central data store offers global access to technology summaries, which are keyed to manufacturing or component system, country of origin, infrastructure requirements, level of investment and feasibility. Every company report that has been published internally or externally is quickly available in many forms. Knowledge-based systems are able to synthesize hundreds of disparate pieces of information, establish patterns and build new learning. Decision-making is quicker.

Through a partnership with a U.S. national laboratory, T4 was able to develop proprietary technology for the building of knowledge. This was a natural extension of the historic relationships, e.g., Toyota had a strategic partnership with Argonne National Laboratories Transportation Technology Research and Development Center since the early 1990's.

Other external environmental factors include economic, infrastructure and competitive forces.

Internal Environment

People

The T4 environment owes a great deal to the family heritage that fostered learning and inculcated values over six generations. The following chart is an abridged family tree.

Tartan Transport Technologies (T3) Heritage (Abridged Family Tree)

Theodore Upson Tartan I (1862-1924)
Manufacturing, Design;
Communications, Supply Management

Charles Prentiss Tartan I
(1887-1958)
Durability and Quality;
Lobbied for Better Roads

Richard Frances Tartan
(1886-1966)
Businessman
Politician

Theodore Upson Tartan II
(1915-1987)
Professional Engineering
Education;
Interest in Miniaturization

Louis Roumell Tartan
(1911-1970)
Statesman

Charles Prentiss Tartan II
(1946-)
Computer Systems Engineer;
Interest in Vehicle Safety

Richard Roumell Tartan
(1936-)
Anthropologist;
Married Yuki Toyoda

Theodore (Trey) Upson Tartan III (1972-)
Design Engineer;
Committed to Community
& Environment

Torri Upson Tartan (1960-)
Manufacturing Engineer;
Business Management

Technical Learning Over a Century

Engineering is deep in the left side of the Tartan Heritage. From Theo Tartan I through Trey, each generation has grown T3's knowledge to address customer needs through technology and engineering capability. Quality, durability, safety and flexibility—each generation has also placed their stamp of personal interest.

Passenger safety through engineering design was a personal interest of Charles (Chipper) Tartan II, resulting in part from the death of his sister-in-law in an automobile accident. Chipper was the first Tartan to understand and leverage computers throughout the company.

Theodore (Trey) Tartan III, CEO of T4, is the creator of the Transport line. Steeped in Tartan's culture and experience, Trey looks to technology to meet the needs of the customer, the company and the community.

Diversity as the Foundation

The right side of the Heritage illustrates the contributions of diversity—professional, educational, racial, religious and gender.

Richard (R.R.) Tartan, an anthropologist and the psychologist, seems at first to be an anomaly in the Tartan clan. The son of a statesman, great grandson of the founder, R.R. applied the family values of disciplined learning to the people side of his work. His value of diversity was shown through his marriage to Yuki Toyoda, descendent of the illustrious Japanese industrialist clan.

Torri Tartan, the CEO of T3, is truly a product of East and West, both genetically and culturally. Her rich racial heritage and business training provide her with skill sets that are highly desirable for a company that must perfect its role in the global community.

Culture

T4 culture is built on 4 values:

Value 1—*Strengthen Relationships through Continuous Learning*

This value supports T4's core competency of customer and employee relationship management, but it also reflects the values of both the Tartan and Toyoda family histories, which have been built on strong familial relationships.

Value 2—*Celebrate the Individual Differences of a Truly Diverse Work Force*

Traditionally, diversity includes race, culture, religion and gender. T3, through the experiences of the Tartan family, is an organization that has learned the value of inclusion and the understanding that diversity brings. The Toyoda family had a similar history. As a result, T4 employees explore, expect and enjoy the uniqueness of individuals, and value their differences.

Value 3—*Sustain the World Community for Future Generations*

T4 reinforces the idea that the world and its inhabitants are not resources and markets to be exploited, but assets to be seen within the context of the business, protected and grown for the betterment of future generations. The Japanese have grasped the concept of the limited nature of resources, and the need to use them wisely. Both the Toyoda and Tartan families have generations of experience making decisions that affect future generations of their families and the communities in which they live.

Value 4—*Be Better Tomorrow than Today*

Value 4 is an affirmation of the value of both people and knowledge. It addresses the individual, in public and private roles; it addresses the community, in a global and local sense; it addresses the products, services and relationships of T4; and it speaks to T4's responsibility to the global community.

Core Competencies

T3 pioneered the use of sensors to electronically measure customer comfort and is now able to utilize this information not only in vehicle design, but in vehicle personalization. Pre-order profiles of customers include height, weight, and body/vehicle interface coordinates on both a primary and secondary driver. The customer information is gathered at the point of sale, where customers define their personal comfort profile in a 2-POD, the design tool adjunct.

T3 took the 2-POD to a new level when it introduced electronic sensors to record information that the customer was unable to articulate: physical comfort and contentment. Initially, privacy issues were a public concern, but in most cases, customers happily gave their electronic comfort profile to Tartan, based on Tartan's reputation in the global community.

The breakthrough for Tartan's proprietary customer knowledge system came when T3 purchased Mitsubishi Electronics, allowing T3 to develop the electronic measurement equipment needed to capture customer contentment at the physiological level.

In exchange for customer knowledge, Toyota brought its production system, process knowledge, and most importantly, its unique understanding of the value of the human system component of the Toyota Production System. Toyota has long known that their production system is supported by an extensive human system.

Long viewed as a strategic strength of Toyota, T3 sees this human systems infrastructure and related discipline, as essential to survival in the new century. This conclusion was apparent, based on T3's family heritage and diversity.

Another T3 first was proprietary DNA (DNAV), a process developed by Tartan to eliminate problems inherent in recycling and environmental accounting. In 2010, transport companies are responsible for their vehicles from cradle to grave. DNAV is a bio-mechanical marker that exists at the molecular level that allows every component of every vehicle to have a unique identity. Originally, the DNAV marker was used only for identification purposes, but the second generation actually added recycling instruction information to an electronic "chip". Electronic tracking not only confirms that appropriate recycling occurs, but also provides asset and personal protection for Tartan vehicle owners.

Remembrances

This scenario was developed for the Group Vice President of Global Strategy at Ford Motor Company, Jim Donaldson in the year 2000. Much of the work at Ford centered within their strategy group but the scenario was never used. Shortly after it was written, Ford went through the Firestone tire crisis and all the work I began came to a halt as the company went into "crisis" mode. Although I never had the opportunity to go back and finish my task, I think that some of the principles of the Tartan work would still be useful for the great grandchildren of Henry Ford.

Chapter 5

2006 Industrial Base Study— Committee on Small Business, U.S. House of Representatives: A Real World Systemic Problem

What follows is the entire report I completed for the U.S. House of Representatives Small Business Committee under the leadership of The Honorable Donald A. Manzullo (R-Il) which required using systems thinking for the ultimate in problem solving for the nation and which led me to think through the need for a national vision and strategy.

Introduction

In March, 2005, The Honorable Donald A. Manzullo, (R-IL), Chairman, U.S. House of Representatives Committee on Small Business hired Dr. Sheila R. Ronis, a systems scientist, to study a matter of supreme national significance—how to strengthen the U.S. industrial base.

Numerous seminars, discussions, conferences, and studies about the defense industrial base have been held across Washington and the nation, especially in the last year, focusing on such critical topics as the decreasing number of science and engineering students, the decline in domestic manufacturing capability, and adequate research and development funding; with each discussion continuing to further this critical debate on the national agenda.

The purpose of this study, however, was not just to have another discussion. This effort has developed a comprehensive look at all of these strategic issues as a whole. Each one is significant by itself, but represents only one piece of a much larger puzzle. Taken in a vacuum, one can only see a partial reason for America's slowly eroding lead in key industries and the inevitable vulnerabilities this causes.

The Theory and the Challenge

Presuming America is to continue playing the lead role in global affairs, we then must address current vulnerabilities, identify policy shortcomings, and devise proactive strategies to strengthen America.

The goal is to lay out a clear, grand strategy and the roles Congress, the Executive branch, and industry must play in order to create necessary change.

The recommendations in this report, using systems science and systems tools, incorporate input from several experts across many disciplines, both scientific and applied.

This effort explored options for maintaining a robust, adequate, and efficient defense industrial base and the ramifications for U.S. policy in the future. The investigator looked at the similarities and differences between free market and controlled competition models, which is the kind of macro-analysis required in systems science.

Systems scientists are trained to look across the entire spectrum of issues and identify their interdependence and interactions to better understand the whole and its behavior.

The military industrial base fits in a context that includes several system layers. First, the U.S. military industrial base is a subsystem of the overall U.S. industrial base. The U.S. industrial base is a subsystem of the overall economy and the U.S. economy is a subsystem of the global economy. Systems are hierarchical. See Figure 5.1.

At the end of World War II, General George C. Marshall said, "We are now concerned with the peace of the entire world, and the peace can only be maintained by the strong." But, how does the United States remain strong? What does that mean in a globalized world? This study attempts to address these fundamental questions.

Figure 5.1

A Systems Approach to Congressional Action

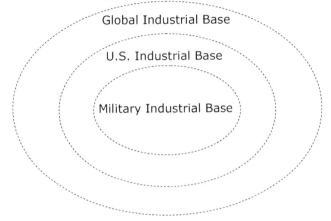

The overall global industrial base is a subsystem of the overall global economy, and finally the global geo-political-economic-military-diplomatic system in which the world operates.

We look at the military industrial base as an element of our national power—the sum total of our country's ability to use our power to shape world events, and ultimately, our national security strategy.

However, the global system is a large, complex, adaptive system in the classic sense, and its non-linearity makes it a "messy" system in the truest sense described by Dr. Russell Ackoff, one of the world's leading authorities in systems science. There is much we can learn about our military industrial system, the impact of global market forces versus those of controlled competition, and issues of public policy by looking at the characteristics of non-linear complex adaptive systems.

There is, at least, another whole set of systems having an impact on our military industrial base. See Figure 5.2. The U.S. military industrial base is a component of the overall National Military Strategy. The National Military Strategy is a component of the overall National Security Strategy. The National Security Strategy is a subsystem of the National Global Strategy that includes foreign policy, global security structures to which the U.S. is a party, trade and offset policies, and so on. Those systems are also hierarchical.

Figure 5.2

A Systems Approach to Congressional Action

U.S. National Global Strategy

National Security Strategy

National Military Strategy

The reality, however, is that both sets of systems exist together, interact with each other and are interdependent. See Figure 5.3. Many questions emerge as we look at these interactive systems, for example:

- Where do our global supply chains fit into these systems?
- Do we know what those supply chains look like?
- Can we track our supply chains throughout the world all the way "down to dirt"?
- Do we really understand the global base well enough to calculate risks associated with the erosion of our domestic industrial base as it relates to national security?

Figure 5.3

A Systems Approach to
Congressional Action

U.S. National Global Strategy
Global Industrial Base

National Security Strategy
U.S. Industrial Base

National Military Strategy
Military Industrial Base

Where do our global supply chains
fit into these systems?

The sets of nested systems from the local to the global are called "globalocalization." It is important that Congressional leaders understand these systems and how they relate to one another. It is also important to make sure that we understand how our industrial base fits into these systems. Globalocalization systems are non-linear, complex, dynamic systems that, if successful, adapt to their environment.

Systems can rarely be controlled, but must be understood in order to influence them. The only way to influence a system is to understand its unique characteristics and capabilities and then act on that knowledge by learning and adapting faster than other competing systems. It is an ironic twist to the competitive advantage of nations. Those that adapt the fastest will win in the end.

Trying to depict systems in order to understand them can get very messy. See Figure 5.4. Although Dr. Ackoff calls these systems "messy," perhaps soup is a better term because the various elements of the many systems interact to meld their flavors, so to speak.

Figure 5.4

To add extra layers of complexity, the messy system has another set of systems added. These are the globalocalization economic, political, diplomatic, and military systems that the United States can influence but not control. The three branches of government, which are both independent and interdependent systems, add another layer of system complexity. Systems science requires integrative mechanisms between elements of the larger system. See Figure 5.5.

The system we are talking about really looks like Figure 5.6, or worse. If we were to really map all the integrative systems, it would be completely black.

Consequently, the challenge facing Congress is to understand the systems nature of the erosion of the U.S. military industrial base and its larger sister, the overall industrial base. National security and the ability to maintain technological leadership and remain a superpower are at stake.

Methodology

After a Roundtable discussion in which experts in science, government, and industry were drawn together, many suggestions and lessons learned were developed. The ideas are separated into what Congress, the Execu-

Figure 5.5

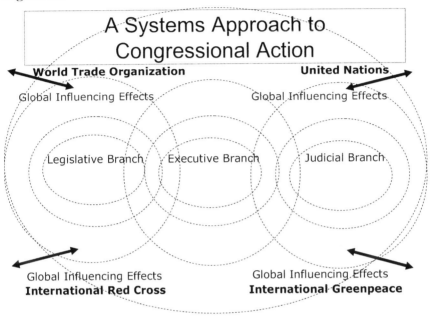

Figure 5.6

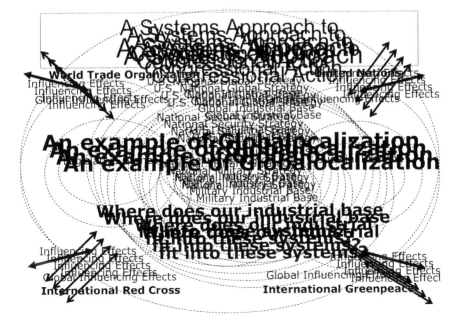

tive Branch, and industry can do to ameliorate the problems associated with erosion of the overall industrial base, and its smaller subsystem, the military industrial base. Special thanks to Larry Smith and Ideation of Southfield, Michigan, for their contribution of the TRIZ tool to aid in the development of causal loop diagrams.

The lessons include the fact that the military industrial base and its supply chain cannot be separated from the other systems. The system can be influenced, but not managed or controlled, despite the fact that federal agencies and departments contribute to the forces on the system.

We have found that the policies and actions of other nations influence our industrial base whether we want them to or not. This includes trade policies like defense trade offsets, which influence our ability to be globally competitive.

While calculating risks across global supply chains needs to be improved, the real question is how do we assist the defense industrial base to reduce its vulnerabilities and remain strong so we can be concerned with the peace of the entire world and remain a superpower?

Assumptions

When scientists undergo a study, it is customary for the principal investigator to disclose any biases or assumptions held by that investigator. The following represents some of those assumptions or biases:

- The forces that are deteriorating and eroding the overall U.S. industrial base will eventually lead to loss of U.S. global superpower status, if the U.S. stops investing in its future capabilities in a systemic way. The defense industrial base is a microcosm of the overall industrial base. The issues leading to offshoring are global competitiveness issues. They include: structural health care costs, legacy pension costs, legacy infrastructure costs, and lack of investment in basic and applied R&D, especially in key manufacturing technologies, both process, as well as product.
- Globalization will continue unabated unless thresholds are developed below which some industrial capability is precluded from being sold or offshored to foreign countries.
- Globalization is not the enemy; lack of its management, however, can create serious vulnerabilities.

- All "foreign" is not the same; just as all allies are not the same . . . some present higher risks than others.
- The warfighter deserves the best in the world. The question is whether the United States will remain the best in the world for those key technologies identified as critical by DoD, or will we be forced to rely on "strategic" partners?
- The U.S., as the lone superpower, is better off for fostering a just international order than the present rising competitors.

Recommendations

The recommendations are provided in three categories; those initiatives appropriate for Congress, the Executive branch, and for industry.

Congressional Initiatives

1. Many of the nation's problems require solutions that are interagency within the Federal Government. This requires the funding of inter-agency missions. Congress should create a new super-committee populated with senior members of all committees of Congress. This committee will develop interagency mission funding mechanisms through inter-committee decision-making processes across governmental boundaries. Systems scientists see the need to break down the barriers in the stovepipes of government from top to bottom.

2. Congress should establish a National Strategy Center housed within National Defense University (NDU) at the Department of Defense. The center will annually produce a *National Strategic Plan* to help senior government and congressional policymakers plan for the future by integrating the economic, diplomatic and military elements of national power and the role the U.S. will play in the future (including how we will remain a superpower). *The National Strategic Plan* will be developed within the context of a visioning center that will continuously develop 360-degree scenarios of the future. This allows policymakers to plan for an integrated future across the entire government spectrum, including Congress.

The *National Strategic Plan* will be considered major guidance to policymakers; not the nation's policy, itself. The establishment of this Center may be the first legislative action of the new cross-governmental committee. The National Strategy Center should be authorized and annually funded by Congress as an independent, nonpartisan institution insulated from political pressures, but able to assist the Executive branch, Congress, and others with research, analysis and information regarding the future direction of the country. Taking into consideration its statutory requirements, the Center will only have two missions: (1) develop an annual National Strategic Plan and (2) educate policy leaders on integration techniques to develop National Grand Strategy.

3. The nation needs to maintain a capability to be globally competitive in product and process innovation. To do that, Congress should fund programs in Commerce and Defense that will regain U.S. manufacturing prowess and leadership across the board. In order to be world leaders, the U.S needs leadership in investment in R&D—nothing else will produce the leading edge knowledge, capabilities, and patents the country must have to remain an economic and military superpower. We must encourage increased investment in manufacturing across government-owned operations, as well. And, as a country, we must learn to manage risks across the supply chains of the military to mitigate the possibility of being blackmailed by any country or transnational threat. The Department of Defense needs to do a statistical analysis of its supply chains down to the very bottom to ensure knowledge of where their supplies are coming from.

4. To be strong and mitigate our global risks, Congress should use funding within the national laboratory system to support the higher education system and U.S. industry to maintain U.S. knowledge and innovation advantages. Congress should find incentives to increase the ability of these labs to cooperate with industry and academia to leverage resources. We are not doing a good job in transferring technology to industry. It's imperative to make the use of Cooperative Research and Development Agreements (CRADAs) much easier. A CRADA is a written agreement between a private company and a government agency to work together on a project. Created as a result of the Stevenson-Wydler Technology Innovation Act of 1980, as amended by the Federal Technology Transfer Act of 1986, a CRADA allows the Federal government and non-Federal partners to optimize their resources, share technical expertise in a protected environment,

share intellectual property emerging from the effort, and expedite the commercialization of federally developed technology. It can:

- Provide incentives that help speed the commercialization of federally-developed technology.
- Protect any proprietary information brought to the CRADA effort by the partner.
- Allow all parties to the CRADA to keep research results emerging from the CRADA confidential and free from disclosure through the Freedom of Information Act for up to 5 years.
- Allow the government and the partner to share patents and patent licenses.
- Permit one partner to retain exclusive rights to a patent or patent license.

The problem with CRADAs has been the contracting mechanisms are long, complicated, and cumbersome, which dissuades companies from engaging in the process.

5. Congress should provide incentives to our most talented young people to become scientists and engineers, linguists, and diplomats.

6. Congress should focus on strategies to improve the nation's energy policies. This would include aggressive funding of alternative fuel research.

7. Congress should rethink U.S. trade, defense offsets, and Committee for Foreign Investment in the U.S. (CFIUS) policies that encourage offshoring of jobs and technologies. Incentives should be devised that encourage the maintenance of high value-added jobs inside the country.

8. Reform of those national systems that are keeping U.S. industry uncompetitive, including pension and health care systems.

Specific Areas of Potential Action

The output of the study included dozens of specific suggested actions for consideration. These actions fell into the following five major categories:

- Technical Competitiveness Issues
- Research & Development and Innovation Issues
- Education Issues
- Trade and CFIUS Issues
- Health Care and Pension Infrastructural Issues

Technical Competitiveness Issues

1. *Convince Wall Street to place more value on long-term investments. Change how performance is rewarded.* Although the quarterly reporting of estimates demanded by Wall Street analysts frequently leads companies in the wrong direction, the SEC should not forbid companies from quarterly earnings reporting. However, there should be a way to encourage corporate long-term planning for publicly-traded companies whose long-term interests should be a concern.

2. *Understand the root causes and results of offshoring jobs.* The Government Accountability Office is currently working on a study. The Department of Commerce also completed a 200 page study this year; however, the only portion released was a 12 page summary that provided no useful information.

3. *Provide additional incentives for capital investments, such as using accelerated depreciation.* Current incentives should be studied to determine effectiveness in increasing productivity.

4. Make it easier for small businesses to gain access to capital by incentivizing equity investment by angel investors.

5. *Facilitate the migration of jobs to low-income areas of the U.S. rather than overseas.* This might be accomplished through a partnership with the National Governors Association. The Department of Commerce can also conduct seminars on how to stay in the U.S. for any company thinking of offshoring.

6. *Use standards as a competitive tool.* Standards are currently used as a non-tariff barrier to trade, which is especially a problem with Europe.

Research & Development and Innovation Issues

1. Develop a National Research Agenda; recruit institutional champions for R&D.
2. Increase overall R&D funding, especially in the physical and biological sciences across the Federal government.
3. Provide incentives for foreign scientists and others who work in science and technology to remain in this country if they have been educated in this country.
4. Request the National Academies of Sciences to benchmark international, states' and regions' science and technology best practices and economic development and share the knowledge.
5. Develop an Advanced Manufacturing/Distributed Manufacturing Initiative at the National Institute of Standards and Technology.
6. Develop incentives to increase the number of science, technology, and engineering students.
7. Improve commercialization processes. Develop a program to accomplish this mission at the National Institute of Standards and Technology.

Education Issues

1. Provide entrepreneurs education in science, technology, and engineering; require Small Business Innovation Research Program (SBIR) awardees to take entrepreneurship/business classes.
2. Improve the "No Child Left Behind" Act to test for preference compatibility in high school. Aid in job placement.
3. Invest in distance learning options to bring university experiences to students; promote on-the-job training and e-learning.
4. Request the Department of Labor to develop new workforce training programs for math and science teachers.

Trade and Committee on Foreign Investment in the U.S. (CFIUS) Issues

1. Congress should consider a mirror policy on defense offsets, with a tariff penalty across the board for currency manipulation.
2. Strengthen the SBIR Phase III program.
3. Develop alternative energy sources and reduce the country's dependency on foreign oil. The Department of Energy and the Department of Defense should increase basic R&D to accomplish this objective.
4. Put pressure on foreign governments to enforce trade laws, especially intellectual property laws. Develop a Grand Strategy for China.
5. Ensure a balance between national security and economic concerns in defense-related policies:
   - CFIUS: lower and broader threshold for investigation
   - Export controls: better focus on targeted technologies/reform process
   - DoD procurement policies: impacts on industrial base must be understood in broader terms
6. Support regulatory reform bill.
7. Improve trade promotion for small and medium-sized businesses.

Health Care Infrastructural Issues

- Strategic industries are disproportionately affected and can't compete
- Workforce participation and productivity are adversely affected
- Strategic non-health investments, public and private, are crowded-out
- Indebtedness to foreigners is fueled by public health care spending
- Our social fabric is threatened by increasing numbers of uninsured
- Majority of uninsured are small business owners and their employees

Problem: Health care spending in the U.S. is much higher than other developed countries and yet our population health lags and we have more uninsured.

Resulting National Priorities: Each of these threats must be addressed as a national priority. We must:

- Ensure that critical industries are not put under by health care costs
- Improve the health of our population—better behaviors and better care
- Improve the efficiency and effectiveness of our health care system
- Determine the appropriate level of public spending and then fund it
- Implement policies that reduce numbers of uninsured

1. Identify industries put at risk by escalating health care costs and develop solutions to ease the burden.

Health care costs affect the survivability of some industries more than others. Industries that are most affected must be identified and individually examined. If particular cases represent a threat to our economic security, steps must be laid out to deal with the threat.

2. Increase funding for the Agency for Healthcare Research and Quality (AHRQ.)

   a. "Research on our health care system can save more lives in the next decade than bench science, research on the genome, stem-cell research, cancer vaccine research, and everything else we hear about on the news . . . there is a gap between what medicine can do and what physicians actually do; the role of health services researchers in this equation is to try and understand how to narrow that gap." (Atul Gawande, Academy Health Reports, September 2005)

   b. "The federal government pays $455 billion for health care in the United States, but devotes only $300 million to the budget of the Agency for Healthcare Research and Quality. More research regarding ways to improve care, eliminate waste and ineffective care, and promote greater efficiency is crucial to improving the performance of the U.S. Health system." (Karen Davis, "Will Consumer Directed Care Improve System Performance?" Commonwealth Fund Issue Brief, August, 2004)

c. AHRQ can fund research that will address a number of the national priorities listed above . . . for example:

1. research into methods for incentivizing healthy behaviors
2. research to support more effective pay for performance schemes
3. research into more cost effective care delivery models (e.g., greater use of lower trained personnel)

d. AHRQ is also the primary federal funding source for health information technology (IT) pilot projects. Health services IT may be the single most important step toward long term improvements in quality and efficiency. It is estimated that health IT can save up to 7.5% of health care costs through its impact on medical errors alone. Broader impacts could save as much as 30%. (David Brailer, "Economic Perspectives on Health Informational Technology," Business Economics, July, 2005. Richard Hillestad, et. al., "Can Electronic Medical Record Systems Transform Health Care? Potential Health Benefits, Savings and Costs," Health Affairs, 24(5):1103-1117.)

3. Create a national institute to assess the effectiveness of drugs, consultations, procedures, and tests.

a. This is a crucial step toward a health care system in which services are delivered and reimbursed based upon scientific evidence as to their effectiveness and value.

b. "A landmark government financed study that compared drugs used to treat schizophrenia has confirmed what many psychiatrists long suspected: newer drugs that are highly promoted and widely prescribed offer few—if any—benefits over older medicines that sell for a fraction of the cost." (*New York Times*, September 20, 2005). The FDA assesses the efficacy of drugs but not their cost effectiveness relative to alternatives.

4. Develop and implement a feasible approach to expanding insurance coverage.

Every year, more and more low wage workers are priced out of private insurance coverage. Some go on Medicaid but most simply go uninsured and without needed services. Many end up in emergency rooms and hospitals with problems that were preventable. This care is largely 'uncompensated' but, in reality, is funded through over-payments by private and . . . to some extent . . . public insurers. Insurance coverage is also becoming at risk for early retirees whose sponsoring companies are near bankruptcy. It is also likely that consumer directed health plans will push up premiums for less healthy individuals and this could push some high users into the uninsured category. The approach favored by many health sector leaders is to provide tax subsidies to low wage workers and to provide an option similar to the Federal Employee Health Benefits Plan (FEHBP).

5. Accelerate investment in information technology for the health care industry.

- Single most effective step toward quality and efficiency
- Interoperable standards
- Education

6. Disease and Health Management must be national system programs.

- National support to improve health, obesity, smoking, exercise, food quality and quantity
- Reduce costs for chronic illness treatment, lowest cost is prescriptions at home
- Reward performance: reward better care, better management and more cost effective outcomes
- Help commercial entities understand and manage health risks, i.e., Pitney Bowes business strategy vs. benefit problem

7. Invest in Health Services Research.

- Government pays $455B in care but only invests $300M in research

- Research in health care system can save more lives/cost than life/bench science in next 10 years
- IT pilots, macro economic models
- What is the "system after next"?

8. Provide Transformational Education.

- Implement an MEP (Manufacturing Extension Partnership) program like model to transfer commercial cost practices to health care providers—especially small, midsized and community health centers
- TQM and continuous improvement
- Lean Six Sigma
- Effective use of IT

9. Implement and reward continuous quality improvement and make results visible to consumers. Healthcare Intelligence Network (HIN) provides health care professionals information on the business of healthcare.

10. Improve the process to accelerate deployment of innovations.

- Industry best practices
- Pilot
- Display
- MEP like accelerators
- Reward productivity gains

11. Workforce training in healthcare is essential.

- More programs are retraining than we are graduating
- Health care employs more people than automotive in Michigan
- Supply demand issue
- Incentive to become doctors
- Need incentives to become nurses/technicians

Special thanks to Ken Baker and Altarum in Ann Arbor, Michigan, for their contributions to the Health Care suggestions.

Executive Branch Initiatives

1. The Executive branch needs to begin to understand and manage the United States as a system. This requires working with Congress to ensure the Grand Strategy requirements of the nation are properly resourced through Congress.
2. The Executive branch needs to acknowledge the problems associated with the erosion of the U.S. industrial base and demonstrate leadership to strengthen the core of U.S. economic prowess.
3. The Executive branch, working through the Department of Commerce International Trade Agency, and Congress must find ways to hold other nations accountable for intellectual property theft. Some of the world's largest companies, including General Motors, are having difficulty winning this war.
4. The Executive branch, working with Congress, must reduce the national budget and trade deficits. No other single action will be as important to the future of this country.

Industry

U.S. industry has many challenges to maintaining global leadership. There are several specific changes that need to be made:

1. U.S. industry needs to stop reporting quarterly earnings estimates. Wall Street must understand the need to invest in the future even when the payback will be years in the making. The current situation encourages no investments in the future, providing no returns in innovation. This is leading many publicly traded companies in the wrong direction, as well as encouraging the offshoring of many jobs, including high value-added jobs.
2. U.S. industry needs to be more aggressive in partnering with governmental institutions at all levels. An increase in the number of Cooperative Research and Development Agreements (CRADAs) with the national laboratories would speed the commercialization of federally developed technology and improve global competitiveness.

3. U.S. industry needs to more accurately calculate the risks associated with global operations in a world of transnational threats, such as, being targeted for disruption across global supply chains.

Issues of such importance as those discussed in this study deserve far more work to develop them further toward solutions. Congress should continue this effort into a Phase II that brings stakeholders into the process for non-partisan discussion.

Remembrances

We have had many positive responses to the study and action plans are just being developed on many fronts. Although this study did not use a strict visioning process, the fact that we focused on using systemic approaches including system draws, I think there are many lessons learned in our simple approach. And, what I learned sets the stage for Chapter 6.

Chapter 6

The National Strategy Center: A Real World Visioning and Strategy Solution

This book has been a description of a visioning process for organizations that need to shape their environments in order to be successful in the 21st Century. Organizations are not the only ones who must develop visions. Countries must as well. In my work with various elements of the U.S. Government, it has become clear that the United States does not have a vision of the future nor a Grand Strategy to get there. The nation needs one now and always will in the future. This chapter describes my journey to that conclusion.

The Department of Defense

My first exposure to the Department of Defense came when my friend and colleague, Sergio Wechsler at GM called me one day in 1989 and said, "Do you know anyone at the U.S. Army? I just met a whole group of people who sound just like you." I told him I knew no one and he explained that he had been invited to participate in the U.S. Army War College's capstone event. Each year, at the end of a one year educational experience, the U.S. Army War College in Carlisle Barracks, Pennsylvania, invites 400 "representative citizens" to spend a week with their graduating class. Sergio was one of those individuals invited. The following year, he nominated me to go and, of course, I went. That event turned out to be life changing. There, I did, indeed, meet many people who thought systemically and strategically—a whole community I did not know. Also there, I met the Commandant, Major General Paul G. Cerjan, who would go on to get his third star and ultimately become the President of the National Defense University. He introduced me to the world of the Pentagon and he and I have been working together ever since.

At the Department of Defense, I had the enormous privilege of working with The Office of the Secretary of Defense (OSD) through the Institute for National Strategic Studies (INSS) at the National Defense University (NDU). It was during the Clinton Administration, and the Secretary of Defense was William Cohen. In that project, my colleagues, the Honorable James R. Locher, III, and Dr. Patrick M. Cronin were involved in looking at a vision of the future of the Department and the national security community during the Defense Reform Initiative.

When I had the opportunity to work with Jim and Patrick, we had a challenging assignment. Jim Locher was officially part of the Defense Reform Task Force. At that time, Patrick was the head of Research at INSS supporting Jim. Defense reform is a very difficult process. It is a political process more than a typical "change" process and that changes your chance of really "pushing the limits." Fortunately, for me, I had just completed *Asimov* when I began to work with both Jim and Patrick; two of the most brilliant men I have ever met. I had the chance of a lifetime to work with and learn from both of them.

Today, after being the Vice President for Research at the United States Institute of Peace, and then, Assistant Administrator for Policy and Program Coordination at the U.S. Agency for International Development (USAID), Patrick Cronin became the Senior Vice President for Research at the Center for Strategic and International Studies (CSIS) in Washington and ultimately, the Director of Studies at one of the world's leading think tanks; the prestigious International Institute for Strategic Studies (IISS) in London. Patrick began his career as a naval officer with a master's degree and doctorate from Oxford and an impressive knowledge of Asia including its languages. Everywhere he goes, he brings his touch of "genius" and pragmatism.

Jim Locher, today, is chairing the Defense Reform Commission in Bosnia and continues to take on the greatest challenges the Pentagon faces at the request of the Secretary or the Chairman of the Joint Chiefs of Staff. Jim, when on the staff of Senator Barry Goldwater, wrote and managed the process of passing the Goldwater-Nichols Act of 1986, the legislation that reorganized the Pentagon and made it "joint." After that, he became the first Assistant Secretary of Defense for Special Operations and Low Intensity Conflict. The senior most leadership at the Pentagon has continually given him difficult assignments and he has continued to perform them brilliantly. His MBA from Harvard has also helped him understand the integration of economics, diplomacy and military capabilities. Both Democrats and Republicans respect his objective understanding of organizational behavior and how best to accomplish a job in a complex and uncertain future. Both Patrick and Jim transformed my thinking about the future of the United States.

Jim, Patrick and I worked on a vision for the future of the Department that could not be separated from the future of the country and the world. The work we did in the 1997 and 1998 time period would have an enormous influence on what would ultimately be an effort with the U.S. House of Representatives.

This past year, I had two privileges. First, the opportunity to work with the Honorable Donald A. Manzullo, (R-Il), Chairman, Small Business Committee of the U.S. House of Representatives and his Chief Counsel, Bradley Knox, to study the national security implications of the erosion of the industrial base. Second, the opportunity to work with the Honorable Suzanne D. Patrick, former Deputy Under Secretary of Defense for Industrial Policy (DUSDIP) to develop a concept of how the United States should develop a national strategy through the establishment of The National Strategy Center.

In my original study for DoD with Jim and Patrick, I found that the lack of a national Grand Strategy was an integral problem for the country in general. My work with the Congress confirmed it. The eroding industrial base was one of many symptoms and so I recommended the creation of The National Strategy Center where interagency processes could be developed, as well as Grand Strategy. My work with Suzanne Patrick reinforced my systemic and strategic thinking pushing the bounds of what exists toward what could exist if the country looked at the second, third and fourth order effects of decisions through the eyes of the integration of economic, diplomatic and military filters.

Suzanne Patrick and I got to know each other when she was the keynote speaker at The Heritage Foundation event that studied the state of the industrial base in early 2005 and I was on the panel of experts who further discussed the issue. She had nearly thirty years of experience in global financial markets, warfighting capabilities, and military intelligence; was a recognized expert in defense industries worldwide and as a

Wall Street investment professional, as well as a military program manager. She also was a Commander in the U.S. Naval Reserve, specializing in intelligence.

Suzanne also was willing to speak on a panel at the Industrial College of the Armed Forces (ICAF) at the National Defense University in Washington. ICAF, under the Command of Major General Francis Wilson was sponsoring, with the U.S. Army, one of their Eisenhower National Security Symposia Series events that I was chairing. The faculty at ICAF includes some of the nation's best thinkers in resourcing national security strategy and teaching strategic leadership in a world of what they call "VUCA" or volatility, uncertainty, complexity and ambiguity.

Suzanne and I realized that we saw the nation and the world in very similar ways though through somewhat different filters. We then spent months studying the feasibility of creating The National Strategy Center that would be a private think tank like no other; that would merge the "storyboarding" disciplined process she had used at the Office of the Secretary of Defense with my visioning process. We created a comprehensive brief and plan of action including vision, values, operating philosophy, budgets, and job descriptions. We even asked our friends at Northrop Grumman TASC to develop a virtual tour and design theme since they had a great deal of experience with the building of leading edge software—hardware interfaces for strategic purposes. Then, we began to talk to the thought leaders of the beltway. We gained many admirers. But, the reality of creating and adequately funding the Center was problematic. This was especially difficult since we were both working on other projects, and I eventually took the position I have at Walsh College in Troy, Michigan and Suzanne was traveling all over the world with her consulting projects. Perhaps our proudest moment though was having General Brent Scowcroft, tell us our ideas were not only good, but that he had tried to do something similar when he was the National Security Advisor to President George H.W. Bush. So, I decided that we should suggest that Congress create the Center, and possibly put it at the National Defense University, especially at a time when the school was preparing to become a National Security University under the Command of now Lt. General Fran Wilson, another brilliant strategic thinker.

I have shared many of my experiences with DoD in these pages. The larger system that DoD is a part of is the National Security community and what *should* be the long term National Strategy of the United States. Without a strong vision of the future and a grand strategy to implement that future, it is unlikely that the United States will be capable of working toward a world of increasing liberty, prosperity or peace. So understanding this issue is literally a matter of war and peace; thus the need for The National Strategy Center.

The question is, "*how* do the broad, systemic relationships in the nation need to work together if the United States is to have a vision of itself in the world and a plan to make it real?" Visioning needs to be accomplished holistically. The future global geopolitical environment and internal environment in the United States both need to be effectively "shaped" in this century of uncertainty and complexity. This requires the development of a new role for the U.S. in the world of the 21st Century.

National Strategy cannot be looked at as "parts of a puzzle." Since we know that to understand a system, you do not break it down into its component parts or only look at the pieces of the puzzle, you must look at the entire mosaic that is created when the pieces fit together and you only see the mosaic in the next larger system.

If the system we are looking at is the holistic, integrated National Strategy of the United States; it will include its foreign policy, economic, diplomatic, military, intelligence, education, healthcare, etc., all of its policies, woven together to create a holistic vision of who we are in the future and how we should get there.

Unfortunately, the United States does not have such a strategy or vision—nor is there any mechanism to develop one anywhere within the federal government. The U.S. simply does not have a decision making process to develop a long term integrated vision of American involvement and strategies in the world or our strategies at home. How can we possibly be effective at shaping our environment, or developing effective plans for shaping, if we have no way to think through the whole, let alone, make decisions about how to engage anywhere in the world. *Can the United States continue to be a world leader if it is always in a reactive mode and never proactive?*

I think not.

Our current national decision making structure is simply inadequate and antiquated for the world we are inheriting in the Post Cold War, Global War on Terrorism, 21st Century.

There will be little ability to secure our homeland, and even less ability to protect American interests around the world, if so much of the world remains in what Tom Barnett calls the "gap" countries (Barnett,

2004). The current state of instability within these countries will not improve without American leadership. That leadership requires a holistic, integrated and, most likely interagency planning and decision-making apparatus that today simply does not exist.

I have traditionally worked with some of our nation's largest global firms, AT&T, General Motors and Ford Motor Company. What is astonishing to me is that each of those organizations, and many others I have been involved with, have what I would call an integrated decision making process that produces an integrated global strategic plan—region by region, country by country, market by market.

Although none of these companies have to deal with any issue as complex as global security or the large scale societal collapse we see in many areas of the world, the models they use to integrate decision making and develop their plans might nevertheless be helpful. Even today, General Motors does business in one form or another in virtually every nation on the planet. A National Security Strategy is on the same scale, though, its execution is far more complex.

Now, General Motors is not a representative democracy, but, in the last decade they have made great strides toward developing processes to listen to their constituents, if you will, their stakeholders, and integrating that input into their global strategies. Having GM listen to their stakeholders to develop their global grand strategies and a vision for the future and having the American government listen to its constituents with the aim of developing global grand strategy and a vision for the future may seem like apples and oranges. But, I think they have more potential similarities than differences. And, more importantly, GM is not the only global company with processes like this. Toyota is one that comes to mind.

One of the most important elements of the corporate process is the development of a joint vision, which represents multiple stakeholders. And, DoD has *some* experience in the development of joint visions.

I do not want you to get the impression that I want to reinvent government. I do not want to change the Constitution or the Bill of Rights. But, our Founding Fathers could not have foreseen the creation by Congress of nearly 300 agencies and departments of the federal government—each of which has a unique mission and has been created in isolation from the others. Each of these agencies should be contributing to the National agenda. They certainly represent the elements of national power. Dr. Deming used to say "a system must have an aim" to be a system.

What is the aim of the United States? Perhaps, we could say, "life, liberty, and the pursuit of happiness," within the system framework of maintaining the Constitution, the Bill of Rights, and providing for a common defense. Of course, another system constraint includes a finite amount of tax dollars and globally competitive capital for free market growth, with which to build the infrastructure and, in addition, the knowledgeable people essential for a society to have effective leadership.

We may want The National Strategy Center to assist in the development of the integrative mechanisms and formal interagency processes and doctrine that we will need to ultimately develop our National Strategy and support our aim. National Strategy is very broad.

We might want to begin by asking each department and agency of the federal government to describe how they support the National Strategy. We should also ask if they support the *National Security Strategy*, and, if so, how. The National Strategy Center would integrate the economic, diplomatic and military elements of national power including recommendations for the *National Security Strategy*. The Center will assist all government officials to improve their decision making ability by providing context since also included in the development of The National Strategic Plan would be the use of the visioning process described in this book. It would be used to explore scenarios of the future and issues that can shape various futures. As a component of the National Strategy process, the visioning process will be useful in developing their plans for accomplishing the National Mission of the United States and its need to engage in shaping the world to accomplish this mission. As a nation, we need a vision of what role we want to play in the world for this new century and how we will improve the security, not only of our homeland, but the world, and American interests in it. There will be no security at home, and there will be no protecting American interests around the world, without a strong America as a superpower.

With the fall of the Berlin Wall in the eighties and the concomitant crumbling infrastructure of the former Soviet Union, with the increasing pace of change and technology and the globalization of the world economy, the stable pre 9-11 world of America has changed forever. These changes now include a Global War on Terrorism that is ambiguous and difficult to fight with a non-state enemy.

Americans require a vision and leadership that will look across the government to optimize national resources to ensure a viable future for

American superpower status to shape the complex, unstable, and sometimes chaotic world.

If we are to be successful at improving the protection of Americans and American interests, we will need to improve our efforts to "shape" the world. Shaping, after all, is a form of influencing events in your favor. But, to know what you want to influence, it is imperative that you have thought through a vision of what role you want to play, first. Influence, in the 21st Century will not be a "U.S. centric" only consideration, but must consider impacts worldwide. In our representative democracy, the idea of defining a new role for the nation needs to be openly discussed and debated.

Defense is a key, but not the only component of National Security; hence, the need to integrate economic and military elements of national power. In fact, the economic assessment should begin the process. The future of National Strategy will depend on a formal interagency process that will need to be developed in much more detail than it currently is. And, *The National Security Strategy of the United States*, published in The White House from time to time needs to become more than a political philosophy or policy wish list. It must become a viable strategic, operational and tactical reality. And, that will require interagency planning, process, doctrine and vision.

The National Strategy, the *National Security Strategy* and the global security of the rest of the world will depend upon the role DoD will play in this process. What role, then, should they play?

Our military forces will be expected to function well along the entire war-peace spectrum of contingencies and operations other than war. We know that many of tomorrow's challenges and opportunities will be precisely because of the amount of continuous change and uncertainty in the world. We also know that there will be many different venues for conflict from deep space to cyber space, from urban areas to deep underground, and within the U.S. homeland as well as around the world. 9-11 taught us that.

There will also be challenges with transnational concerns such as Al Qaeda that involve intertwined economies, mass migration, drug trade, organized crime and the environment. The internet age continues to reduce the timelines to react or recover, with instant global communications, information access and advanced technologies. Our fanatical adversaries from rogue states, terrorist groups and non-state actors will attack us in asymmetric ways using their strengths against our weaknesses using whatever is at their disposal from high technology information warfare, to weapons of mass destruction.

"Traditional" warlike conflicts will be reduced and replaced with far more difficult to defend conflicts. And, no matter what kind of conflicts we are engaged in, we will rarely be acting alone. Most of the time, DoD will be working in concert with additional partners such as other government agencies in an inter-agency mode, allies, coalitions, ad-hoc partners, non-government institutions, such as global corporations, and non-governmental organizations, such as the Red Cross.

We will be most effective if we are shaping the future. But, how do we shape? Only through preparedness and shaping can a more stable world emerge. This will ultimately rely upon cooperative security arrangements around the world based on mutual trust and collective planning. But, when this fails, we must be able to be ready, capable, and agile enough to fight and win the nation's wars, whatever they may look like.

These issues are not only the purview of the military. They are the responsibility of the entire National Community—and that community is very broad. Yet, it is that broad community that needs to develop a vision of the future. Once we have a vision, we will need to think about *how* to shape the future of the world. We will need a global strategy; region by region, country by country, including our own—and integrated across the economic, diplomatic and military elements of national power.

Internally, there needs to be a mechanism to bring the diverse agencies involved in National Strategy together to develop a joint vision and a plan to carry it out. In fact, if a formal interagency process is not voluntarily developed, there is a chance that it will be imposed by Congress in legislation that will "force" agencies to work together, not unlike the Goldwater-Nichols Act, which forced the jointness activities between the services. But, there is a strong possibility that the legislation may not be developed by someone as wise as my friend and colleague Jim Locher, whose genius enabled the Goldwater-Nichols Act to be successful.

After personally experiencing the divestiture and reorganization of the old Bell System and the telecommunications industry in this country, I firmly believe that to create the rules of play is far superior to having those rules imposed upon you by those who may not understand all the fundamental functions. And, yet, this is exactly what could happen if the federal agencies that need to work together cooperatively can not learn how to develop effective formal processes to integrate the diverse elements to carry out a National Strategy; potentially to develop interagency doctrine, strategic, operating, and tactical plans.

Earlier, I said that after World War II, General George C. Marshall said,

> We are now concerned with the peace of the entire world. And the peace can only be maintained by the strong. (Marshall, 1945)

These words are as true today as ever. But, what does it mean for the United States to be strong in the 21st Century? The National Security community must be thought of from a "systems" perspective in order to enable the United States to be strong and secure . . . and far beyond defense issues, but economic and diplomatic capabilities. Systems have interdependent and interconnected elements, and the National Strategy will reflect that. If we were to develop a vision in The National Strategy Center to prepare for shaping our environments, what might some preliminary assumptions look like?

- The world is a system. In a system, every element is interdependent with every other element and the system is only as strong as its weakest link.
- The United States has global interests. Its National Strategy needs to include the political, economic, diplomatic, military and other communities inside the government and outside of the government, its citizens, other governments, Non-Government Organizations, global businesses and so on.
- National Strategy also depends upon the education of future generations, at home and around the world.
- Conflict anywhere on the planet can negatively affect the world anywhere, because the world is a system. Therefore, our interests may require U.S. involvement anywhere to deter, reduce or eliminate conflict.
- The process of deterrence, management and reduction of conflicts throughout the world is a value of the United States. Promotion of peace, another value, requires active shaping; in order to prevent, reduce and manage conflict, including post conflict maintenance processes. These are all systemic and they are expensive, but, cost effective in the long run.

- The "rule of law" and principles of good governance are values of the United States and need to be articulated and promoted.

- Peace can only be maintained by the strong, but the National Will may not necessarily provide many more resources to the defense community, especially without an understanding of the realities of the dangers in the world.

An important element emerging from a visioning process may be the understanding that peace prospects and root causes of conflicts are complex and systemic. They require a thorough understanding of the system relationships between elements of a society that can lead to conflict, if not in balance. This may lead to activities to promote peaceful futures through *prevention* on a global basis. That will be the essence of shaping. Prevention is far less costly in dollars and lives than any conflict.

The vision is then developed by looking into the future and deciding what the "system" should look like in an idealistic, but realistic future, including a determination of what the geo-political realities of the world could be if we are actively shaping it. This may include increased roles for the intelligence community in a post 9-11 era that more effectively monitor the dangerous world that has emerged.

Assumptions are made by identifying trends and developing a wide range of alternative futures. This helps us to think through potential roles that the nation will need to play in the various future states. This is important because strategies for action to try and "shape" the desired future become a regular part of the on-going plan.

Since visions are descriptions of the "state of being" in the future with regard to a system's stakeholders, a vision will account for uncertainties. It will look at its stakeholders, such as government partners, other departments and government agencies, internal and external customers, employees, contractors, the general public, the press, Congress, The White House, and so on. One question to be answered is, "what will the National Strategy mean in the eyes of these stakeholders?"

The country needs to define its role in the world for this new century. It needs to refine the shaping policies around the global geopolitical situation, and think through a long term foreign policy. As these emerge, the National Strategy for the 21st Century will co-evolve with all of these efforts. Ideally, they will all be done in a holistic environment that makes sense for the people of the country in The National Strategy Center.

As The National Strategy Center does its work, I would expect some agencies and departments to change their missions and visions. It might be possible to see broader missions and visions emerging.

I could easily imagine reading a new mission statement of the Department of Defense that says:

The mission of the Department of Defense needs to more clearly reflect 21st Century challenges and better support the National Security and National Strategy of the United States by:

- *preventing conflict and deterring potential adversaries,*
- *supporting worldwide stability,*
- *maintaining ready forces for employment worldwide,*
- *responding to threats and protecting U.S. citizens, property and interests,*
- *responding to domestic emergencies and humanitarian assistance at home and abroad,*
- *contributing to other National priorities, and foreign policy*

through cooperation with allies, friends, and other federal and state agencies.

The mission would describe what the Department of Defense is striving for within the context of the National Strategy. The vision would describe what the Department of Defense should become in this new century in a national security context and the context of the National Strategy.

What might such a vision look like?

The vision of the U.S. Department of Defense beyond 2025 might become to support the National Security of the United States and its military, diplomatic, political, economic, social, technological, foreign and domestic policy efforts in the 21st Century by being able to:

- remain premier in its capacity to prevent, deter, and win the nation's wars worldwide, quickly and decisively, in concert with its allies and friends, or unilaterally, with minimum casualties,
- leverage national assets wherever they are, to support national interests, competitiveness, sustainability and capabilities,

- employ superior human resources in both the military and civilian workforce,
- be proactive and work closely and effectively with other federal and state agencies and others to meet dynamic National Security priorities in support of domestic needs and global contingencies,
- be foremost in innovative practices in all areas; leveraging of U.S. core competencies; and efficient stewardship of all resources and capabilities through partnerships with industry, academia and national laboratories to renew the nation's infrastructure while enhancing the overall National Security posture, and be the world leader in information dominance and technological superiority.

The vision would also describe the values of the enterprise, and its overall system, suggesting that the values of the American People must reflect the values of the Department. Those values will include a culture within DoD which will: empower people, reward innovation, encourage teamwork, enhance individual skills, leverage core competencies, provide a safe and healthy workplace, employ contemporary management practices, and instill commitment to excellence.

Ultimately, the vision of the Department of Defense will need "to provide for the common defense while supporting the *National Security and National Strategy of the United States.*"

The vision of the nation may become "to work toward a world of liberty, prosperity and peace in a 21st Century world which should be shaped to our advantage and which supports our national values."

If every organization in the nation, as well as the government develops a vision and a timeline into the future, our children and theirs might inherit a more hopeful and peaceful world in which the United States remains a strong force for good.

Appendix

Accelerated Learning Cycles: Organizational Prerequisites for the Development of a Vision

As the events of September 11 continue to be dissected for lessons learned, some clear patterns have emerged. One of the most important is the need for intelligence that is timely and used. The United States intelligence failures that permitted the attacks on this country are now slowly being addressed, but the mistakes made at the end of the Cold War cost this country a terrible price. *The fates of organizations, as well as countries are tied to their intelligence gathering and using capability. Visioning requires a lot of intelligence and continuous learning cycles.*

Guess what organization in the world, long before the internet's arrival, was found to send half a million messages a day from just one country to its home base via satellite? The CIA? The Israelis? The Russians? Toyota?

If you guessed Toyota, you would be right. As unlikely as it sounds, a study in the late eighties found that Toyota sent over 500,000 messages (the cable traffic) a day from its Torrance, California facility to Tokyo via an encrypted satellite hookup. (Dougherty, 1991). We know that our CIA sent about half as many messages *around the world per day at that time*, and although the Russians' intelligence was still top notch in the early nineties, its infrastructure didn't compare to that of Toyota's.

While I was working with GM, they were going through an "envisioning" experiment using a version of the Royal Dutch Shell visioning process described at length in the book *The Art of the Long View* by Peter

Schwartz (Schwartz, 1991) and *The Living Company* by Arie De Geus (DeGeus, 1997). In the Shell process, four scenarios are explored at the extremes of two variables that explore the most important elements to learn about. For example, a scenario where the world becomes extremely environmentally conscious and highly legislated vs. a scenario in which environmental activities are perceived as less important. Shell, however, had a lot of trouble taking the lessons learned and applying them to the daily decision making process of running the business. Knowing this, GM tried to develop ideas to help them use the insights gained. They were somewhat more successful than Shell, but I went looking for a better model of diffusion of thought and practices and found it at Toyota in Japan.

My friend and colleague, the late Air Force Colonel Andrew Dougherty had worked for the intelligence community in the late eighties before the age of the internet on a project studying the Japanese telecommunications systems; political, economic, military, etc., when he came across an interesting phenomenon. Toyota's cable traffic was about the same amount per day from their Torrance, California encrypted up-link to a satellite that down-linked to Toyota City as the CIA had per day around the world. What on earth were they communicating about? After a lengthy study, he found that the Toyota employees in the U.S. studied all kinds of phenomena to help their Japanese leaders better understand what motivated Americans. About the same time, I was trying to understand what Toyota was doing to better understand their ability to design, engineer and assemble cars so well. Of course, I knew about their mentor and tutor, Dr. Deming, because he was also mine, but I also knew they were taking the P-D-S-A cycle to some level I had never seen before.

Visioning is about learning enough about the world to help you make decisions that will shape the world you want. It is about what the beltway folks call "grand strategy." Everything is looked at "in the context of everything else" as Tom Barnett would say (Barnett, 2004). The engineers at Toyota learned about everything. They knew that their knowledge of the American mind and culture was limited, so they decided they better study everything American. I found Toyota engineers studying all over the world; not just America, but every country they went into. But, the Japanese engineers don't only study automobiles and the auto industry. They study everything! They are the quintessential students. Although this is a story about Japan, other countries have learned their lessons from Japan and Toyota well—the Koreans and the Chinese. As you read about my observations, know that I am now seeing others emulate the Japanese model, as well.

The Japanese have a near obsession with the gathering of information and translating it into intelligence. In their eyes, there can never be too much data. Nor are they at all uncomfortable with data that is vague or even conflicting. It is not at all unusual for a Japanese company to contract with multiple firms of various national origins to do the same study in order to better understand the nature of the customer, as well as the nature of national bias on the research process.

In my travels around the world including Japan, I have seen evidence of the insatiable appetite for strategically gathered information. One sees Japanese engineers at every global auto show, working in pairs, touching, measuring, photographing and analyzing every aspect of competitive products; from frames to finish, from window mechanisms to wiper assemblies.

Learning, education and reverence for knowledge are values which pervade Japanese culture. They view these values as their competitive advantages in the global battles to survive. They believe survival requires control of knowledge which will lead to global domination economically. And, their ability to apply this knowledge, through the development of process, is legendary.

In Paris, I observed them everywhere, studying the picky French consumer. In Sydney and Melbourne, I witnessed the sale of downtown Australian property to the Japanese because they have discovered its value. In Frankfort, they were studying German engineering and banking. In Geneva, I saw them devouring the library of the General Agreements on Tariffs and Trade, known as GATT, before the days of the World Trade Organization. In Zurich they were pursuing economic alliances and a whole lot more.

In Switzerland, they were on an accelerated learning curve. Switzerland is especially interesting to the Japanese because, in many ways, Japan and Switzerland are similar. They both are world class strategists, have a strong and pervasive militaristic history, are nationally chauvinistic, are physically isolated, have amongst the highest per capita incomes in the world, have been accused of ruthless trade dealings, sometimes to the point of being unethical, have carefully managed mid- and long-term strategic plans for social, industrial, technological, and economic development, are a people who are willing to die to defend their country and are masters of illusion in many ways.

But, unlike Japan, Switzerland is not homogenous in culture or race. With its ethnic diversity and four national languages, the Swiss success with the management of cultural diversity is a subject that the Japanese recognize they must master in order to achieve their goals.

I have noticed that one of the Japanese techniques to learn about cultural differences is to study a national institution which reflects a nation's values, norms and behaviors. In Switzerland, for example, I found them studying the Swiss Army documented in John McPhee's *La Place de la Concorde Suisse*! (McPhee, 1984). Why, you might ask, would the Japanese want to study the Swiss Army? Do the Swiss have leading edge technologies? Or advanced weaponry?

Of course, they don't. Their real target for study is the Swiss Army's ability to effectively manage diversity. And the Japanese know that it will be one of the skill sets essential for mastery to achieve global economic success.

I saw them pursuing this quest in Brussels as well as Switzerland. Japanese businessmen were in the offices of the European Community, lobbying as they do in Washington, gathering information on the rules of play for this mega-market. Make no mistake. These are samurai warriors in pin-striped suits on an economic battlefield. The Japanese have a plan to win in the global marketplace.

Brussels is not only the capital of Belgium, it is also the capital of the European community. Belgium is a country that is steeped in multi-lingual tradition, much like Switzerland. French, Flemish, and German are all equally recognized national languages. Over the past several decades, English, as well as other European languages have found their way into the local commercial repertoire. Most recently, Japanese has been added to the signage, even to the menus at restaurants.

Japanese businessmen were very much in evidence in the political and tourist districts of Brussels. Newspapers, brochures and documents are increasingly available in Japanese. The Japanese presence in Brussels is a symbol of national strategic intent. But, the Japanese are found throughout Europe and are in Europe to stay. I have seen them on the trains, on the streets, in the markets, in the restaurants, and of course, at auto shows. Wherever they go, they go to study, to learn, and ultimately, to master. In U.S. terms, every Japanese citizen is a spy.

Even more important than the political and economic rules of the marketplace, the Japanese seek information about customer needs and expectations. Street width, garage size, nature of terrain, lifestyle issues, and many more elements, both hard and soft, are closely monitored. Often this research is conducted in ways foreign to the U.S. approach. For example, to understand the concept of luxury, essential to understanding the voice of the luxury market, one Japanese company studied perfume factories in France. They have listened to their targeted customers in every language, and, in many ways; linguistic, cultural, geographic, psychographic, demographic or economic.

They ask every question imaginable, and then listen.

Their ability to listen to and interact with the voice of the customer is unsurpassed. But their definition of customer has been broadly defined for decades. It is only in recent times that Westerners have thought about customers inside and outside their companies. For many years, they only thought of the ultimate customer who buys their product. The Japanese know that a customer is defined as the individual or team receiving the outputs of their efforts, no matter where in the process they happen to be. And, that broader definition of customer is now being studied to push the boundaries of the next paradigm of customer satisfaction in Japan.

We in the West have tended to listen to our customers differently than the Japanese have and through Western filters.

Because the Japanese listen differently than Westerners, in the product development process, much of that difference is a function of who is doing the listening. Engineers do the listening in Japan. They do the research, both primary and secondary. They populate most of the functions that are involved with the vehicle development process. At Honda, I was told that almost all market research at Honda is done by the vehicle team which is composed of engineers and that the design engineers conduct the research themselves. This is how the voice of the customer is clearly communicated to the mind of the engineer, so that his knowledge of what is possible may end up in the product, giving the customers more than they expect.

At Toyota, this situation is similar. The shusa, or strong program manager/chief engineer, works with his multi-functional team of trained engineers, who also has responsibility for direct discussions with customers.

The translation of customer needs into product occurs through the development of processes that design, engineer, manufacture and sell vehicles. The Japanese are masters at process development, implementation and improvement. Since the days that Dr. Deming came to help them after World War II, they have understood the complexities of process development in the system. The Japanese understand the difference between process and management, how essential they both are, but how very different.

Processes are to be documented, measured statistically and controlled. People are to be managed through leadership. This is what successful companies do. Control of people is inherently the enemy of process because it precludes the energy, intrinsic motivation, ideas and commitment of people from improving the process through learning. And, in Japan, this is considered an irresponsible waste of human resources. The knowledge in the heads of their people is the most important asset any company has.

But this process difference does not fully explain the profound differences in the way the two cultures, East and West listen. The easiest way to discuss these differences is to take a short detour, to a discussion of Japanese religions and how they are different from Western ones, for therein lies insight into a fundamental difference between East and West.

There are many religions in Japan. Hundreds of them. In fact, every small town has some festival in honor of the local gods or faith. Only Buddhism and Shinto are national religions in a true sense. This is important and completely foreign to Westerners where religion is fragmented and each sect is exclusive. In Japan the faiths co-exist. Virtually every Buddhist Temple has a Shinto Shrine cohabiting its property. Happy occasions warrant a trip to the Shinto shrine where birthdays, weddings and births are celebrated. The Buddhist Temple is the destination for unhappy events, to pray for those who are ill, to mourn for a still-born or aborted child, to bury a loved one.

Both faiths are filled with contradictions, superstitions and ritual. Buddhism and the Shinto faith are contradictory in their philosophies, but both are accepted by virtually all Japanese people. Both faiths are at once rigid and forgiving. Both have room for the local simple blind faith and the intellectual wisdom of Confucius. Both have the backing of the people, the government and the corporations.

As you can see, the Japanese have enormous cultural tolerance for ambiguity, for duality, for fuzziness. This is distinctively Japanese, and it has to do with how they listen, learn and communicate. Western thought has trained us to classify information in binary terms, right or wrong, black or white. The Japanese believe in and are comfortable with shades of gray.

Interestingly, it is Buddhism, originally foreign to Japan, which captured the imagination and loyalty of the upper classes during the feudal years during which time it became singularly Japanese in nature. At the same time, the Shinto faith was practiced by the uneducated masses, absorbing local, regional and foreign influences, and changing over time.

Changing philosophies to meet changing needs and adapting to those changes is at the heart of what is Japanese. It requires a learning environment and the continuous asking of questions. Here are a few of the questions being studied by Toyota, Nissan, Honda and others in their efforts to optimize their internal processes through the satisfaction of internal and external customers:

- How do people learn and how is learning enabled?
- What is the optimum size of a team for different tasks?
- How are people motivated?
- What makes people want to work in plants when they have alternatives?
- What will motivate the best and the brightest to relocate to places like Kyushu, the Peoples' Republic of China, or the United States?

Questions like these are at the core of the experiments being conducted in Japan to look at the next paradigms of manufacturing. Many years ago, I had the chance to watch this learning process at the Nissan and Toyota plants in Kyushu, Japan, not far from Fukuoka. Both plants are lean, flexible, agile, customized and capable of production, trying to approach an N of 1, that is, a unique car. Teamwork, trust and control of their processes, brought them to this point. At the time, I was astonished at what I saw. It led me to a better understanding of their learning processes.

At the time of my visit, both plants were state-of-the-art facilities in every way. I witnessed very impressive displays of robotics at every step of manufacturing. Harmony is clearly a "people value" that is cherished. Harmony is at the basis of teamwork, of respect for people. Toyota and Nissan went to great lengths to provide harmony in its many forms. Harmony with the environment, which has been a recurring theme of Japanese auto show displays, is evidenced by Toyota's "Clean Center" which ensures that the waste that is currently necessary to the production of automobiles, does not mar or pollute Kyushu, famed for its rural splendor. Nissan uses water-soluble paints for the same reason. Toyota and Nissan create harmony with their fellow citizens by respecting their environment.

Employees and their on-the-job comfort are major priorities and the plant designs consider all the senses. Human comfort was improved through ergonomic considerations in the lines: adjustable heights and people-friendly controls. Rubber rollers replaced metal ones to reduce noise pollution. Heat-generating operations were placed on the second stories, so as to reduce climatic discomfort wherever possible. Every opportunity was made to make the work environment attractive, with shore-line views in the comfortable dining rooms at both Toyota and Nissan.

Some people perceived these plants to be white elephants, because they provided unneeded capacity. But it is my suspicion, derived from direct feedback at both Kyushu plants, that these facilities were created with the intent of experimenting with several emerging paradigms. These included:

- pushing the limits of team behaviors—and people systems in general—how can a person's contribution to the organization be optimized at every level and in every job?
- environmental responsibility: what are the limits, what are the variables and how can environmental objectives be accomplished in a cost effective manner?
- agile manufacturing processes: how can production of any one type of vehicle be accomplished to be adjusted to market demand—even reduced to a volume of one?

Toyota Kyushu is a wholly-owned subsidiary of Toyota Motor Corporation—not an operating division. Why do you think that is? I think it is because Toyota wants to experiment on a system level—at the level of a strategic business unit, if you will. Otherwise, data may be misleading, and the last thing Toyota wants is to learn the wrong lesson.

It is clear that all of these paradigms are being studied by Nissan and Toyota in Kyushu. However, the highest level of harmony in evidence was demonstrated by the teamwork apparent between Toyota and Nissan—for our visit. Here is a unique harmony indeed: between competitors. I spent the entire day in the company of Japan's two largest auto companies, and it was impossible to tell where planning of one company stopped and the other began. In fact, even the translator we had at Nissan continued with us on to the Toyota plant.

There are many elements of this teamwork which are interesting. Because these are "greenfield" plants and far away from the traditional industrial centers of Japan, we asked about their just-in-time systems. Were suppliers building facilities to service both plants? What other ways were they able to assist their supplier partners? The answers I received from both Toyota and Nissan intimated that they were even sharing common components—but they wouldn't tell me which ones.

Let me be clear, lest you misunderstand my meaning. I am NOT suggesting that Nissan and Toyota are anything other than competitive with one another. They are fierce, acknowledged competitors. But they recognize the importance of partnership on the global battlefield, and they have seamlessly joined forces on those fronts. The Japanese battle to be won the day I visited these plants was to convince the Society of Automotive Analysts and their Wall Street representatives that the Japanese automotive industry is strong, despite the problems with their economy.

And, by and large, the Japanese were successful. They still are, along with those who have emulated them from China and Korea.

Today, many intelligence experts believe that Toyota's intelligence capabilities are still superior to those of any global power. That's because Toyota represents an organization filled with learners who share their knowledge and apply it to improve their day-to-day capabilities.

What does this mean to executives in a large organization?

Toyota is known in many circles as the best institutional learning machine on the planet. They are fabulous at it—even some country's intelligence agencies have benchmarked them.

Why, you might ask, does that matter?

The organizations that learn the best and the fastest and apply that knowledge will be the organizations that win in the global competitive wars in the 21st century.

When a Toyota engineer learns something new, he shares that new knowledge with his company and new knowledge spreads very quickly. That knowledge is incorporated into decision-making and acted upon with lightening speed.

That makes Toyota very different from most Western institutions—companies, governments or academia . . . where knowledge is perceived as the power to get ahead over your colleague in the next cubicle; not a way for the company to get ahead over your competitors across the street or on the other side of the world. Toyota knows who the "enemy" is.

I believe that Toyota employees have adopted the methodologies of the ancient Chinese philosopher Sun Tzu. More than 2500 years ago, he said, in his book, *The Art of War,* (Tzu, 1963 Griffith translation) you must know the enemy and yourself. Although originally meant to offer wisdom for generals, this principle is relevant to today's global competitive wars. In fact, many would call this process global intelligence: the gathering, analyzing, synthesizing and using information to make better decisions and take better actions.

Organizations in competitive situations need this capability. All organizations need to be engaged in routine intelligence work in those areas of the world and in technologies that directly affect their interests and well-being. An organization's very survival requires that they know enough to adapt themselves to accommodate to changes in their environments.

The more adaptive the organization, the more it can easily change and be proactive. If a company can produce learning processes to anticipate what will be changing in the environment, it can plan, sometimes predict, and therefore be ready for or actually *lead* any changes to the environment. It's what the Department of Defense and the CIA call "shaping." To do that, you need to understand your strengths and weaknesses and your competitors, because wars are won by strategizing how to use your strengths against your enemies' weaknesses. This is true for marketplace wars, too. The better and faster you learn about your world the less likely you will be surprised or "paradigmed."

If your organization doesn't have an intelligence capability, they need to begin by studying Toyota. Without needed intelligence, any organization, company or country is at risk . . . it can mean the difference between winning and losing . . . the difference between life and death. We, in the United States all saw the effects of poor intelligence processes on September 11. So visioning needs intelligence or a way to learn; and learning begins by gathering, analyzing and synthesizing knowledge.

Before we move on to describe the accelerated learning cycle, there is one more point. I'm sure you know what a bonsai tree is. Did you know that, on the occasion of the Bicentennial of the United States, the Japanese government sent a gift of two ancient bonsai trees to our country, planted in 1776.

There are many gifts from other nations that were more exotic. Others that were more inherently valuable. Some that had more direct ties to the founding of our nation. But none so symbolic as the bonsai. This gift tells so much about the giver, the receiver and the relationship between the two. First of all, bonsai are very highly valued in Japan. The gift, from the Japanese perspective, was of the highest order. These miniaturized landscapes symbolize Japan, the small island nation with its reverence for nature. The Bonsai also symbolizes the profound patience of the Japanese people who plant seeds in one century, nurture them in the next, and reap the harvest two centuries later. This is the ultimate long-term planning. You may think this anecdote is whimsical, but understand that every Japanese organization has a long-range plan. When I say long range, I mean more than 50 years. Japan has had a 100 year plan, beginning long before the Meiji restoration. They still do. And, so does Toyota, even if they are not published for all to see.

Successful strategy cannot take place in the present. Strategy needs room and time. Short-term "strategies" are merely reactive to the conditions of the hour. Only in the long-term, can you trade off short-term profits, for example, for long-term gains.

All organizations need to improve planning processes for things unforeseen. The global nature of the world demands it. Organizations must become strategic in everything they do, because the penalty for failure is so high.

Organizations need to be clear on who they are and who they want to become. They need to understand their strengths, weaknesses and the environment that is relevant to them. They must be clear on where they want to go and have a strong vision and strong leadership that directs that vision. They must see the big picture in the context of a long time horizon, because that picture drives all activities. The visioning process described in this book is a major contributor to the definition of the vision the organization must develop. But, to really be successful, an organization must be into learning—not knowing. To prepare for visioning, an organization needs to be generating and utilizing knowledge; they need to have an accelerated learning cycle process.

Let us take a look at the learning cycle I put together from studying the way in which Toyota synthesizes its knowledge and turns it into decision making and action following Dr. Deming's P-D-S-A cycle on a corporate system level.

If you look at Figure A1, you will see what looks like a circle. It is not. It is, in fact a spiral, up, out of the page so when you go through all of the steps in the learning cycle, you are in fact above the page. Each time around the circle and you are farther and farther from where you began.

The process is divided into four quadrants. The first, I call the Intelligence Process Quadrant, the second is the Corporate Learning and Memory Quadrant, the third is the Paradigm Shifting Quadrant and the fourth is the Application Quadrant. The x and y axis represent the separators of each quadrant.

The Intelligence Quadrant consists of five steps.

First of all is the data collection phase. This is the step where the organization develops processes to scan the relevant environment for data that it needs to make the day to day, as well as strategic decisions that manage the organization. In most organizations, this step includes the entire environmental scanning process for political, economic, societal and technological trends that effect the organization. In governmental organizations, there can also be military, diplomatic, foreign and economic policy implications for the city, state or province, region, country, and world. Once data are collected, it must be analyzed. What do the data say? In fact, patterns need to be looked for so information is created. Multiple "dots" are connected and a story should emerge. By "synthesizing" the data or putting all the dots into a picture, intelligence should emerge which puts the information into a context or perspective. This is how knowledge is created.

The Corporate Learning and Memory Quadrant has five steps. These begin with knowledge awareness. Once an organization becomes aware of something new, the question, "what does this mean to us?" should be asked and answered. This helps to develop an understanding of the new "quanta" or packet of knowledge that is being studied within its context. When something new is finally understood, acceptance of the new "truth" is important. If people don't agree, most of the time, the new "truth" is then tested out to make sure it fits into whatever prevailing theories exist. A theory is a hypothesis or question about something that may be true, but needs to be tested. The question, "is it a new paradigm?" is asked. Before it leaves the Corporate Learning and Memory Quadrant, it becomes what Dr. Deming used to describe as "profound knowledge," to his students. That is, a phenomena that is well understood because it has been studied and tested using the P-D-S-A cycle against theory, using appropriate data. Profound knowledge is what most people would call wisdom based on scientific methodologies and testing, not experience alone.

Figure A1

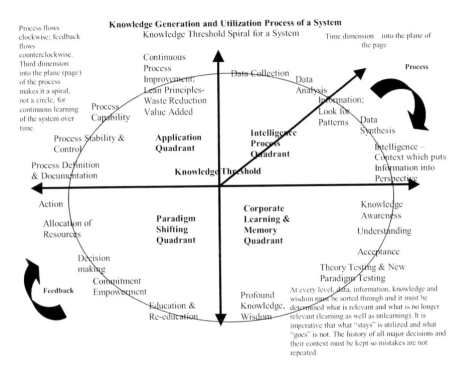

The Paradigm Shifting Quadrant changes the way the organization does everything through education and/or re-education, commitment, empowerment, decision making and an allocation of resources or a real-location of resources. Once an organization goes through these steps, it rarely goes backwards and unlearns lessons once learned. Every once in a while, an organization needs to unlearn something if an organization once learned something that is now wrong. Then, it needs to correct itself through a re-education process. Education includes the process of giving new information to the people of the organizations, as well as educating all stakeholders. This can include the general public, custom-ers, the press, and Wall Street for publicly traded companies. The organization's leaders need commitment to the new knowledge if it will be successful in empowering the organization to use it. Once people feel empowered to use the new knowledge many decisions are made on how it will be used. When decisions are made about integrating some new knowledge area into the way business is conducted, there is a high probability that resources need to be allocated to change something. Decisions aren't decisions unless resources accompany them to implement the decision. Otherwise, no action occurs. There are too many organizations that give lip service to various decisions only to make them meaningless by not attaching the requisite dollars to carry them out. This not only happens in the GMs and Fords of this world, it also happens in Congress!

Finally, the Application Quadrant creates permanent change as the accepted way of managing the organization. All new knowledge is applied as the way to get things done in the organization. But, because the learning cycle never stops, nothing is permanent but the constant changes required through the learning process. Nevertheless, this quadrant has four steps that begin with process definition and documentation. When new knowledge is diffused throughout an organization, it generally needs to be incorporated in the processes that people use in the day to day running of the organization. Those of you who are familiar with the lean quality principles in manufacturing will understand the process cycles of documenting a process, stabilizing it by bringing it into control, usually statistically, measuring the process capability to ensure it is in fact an improvement. Finally, the continuous process improvement cycle keeps processes improving as long as possible.

But, this is not a book about lean principles. Anyone interested in this literature might begin by reading the work of the late W. Edwards Deming. His famous book, *Out of the Crisis*, is a must. (Deming, 1986) Everyone at Toyota reads it.

Bibliography

Ackoff, Russell L, *The Democratic Corporation*, Oxford University Press, New York, 1994.

Barnett, Thomas P.M., *The Pentagon's New Map: War and Peace in the Twenty-First Century*, G.P. Putnam's Sons, New York, 2004.

Biefeld-Brown Effect, http://www.blazelabs.com/f-biefeld.asp, 2006.

Biefeld-Brown Effect, http://jnaudin.free.fr/html/nasarep.htm, 2006.

Brzezinski, Zbigniew, *The Grand Chessboard: American Primacy and Its Geostrategic Imperatives*, Basic Books, New York 1997.

Buckley, Walter, Ed., *Modern Systems Research for the Behavioral Scientist: A Sourcebook for the Application of General Systems Theory to the Study of Human Behavior*, Aldine Publishing Company, Chicago, 1968.

Capra, Fritjof, *The Turning Point: Science, Society and the Rising Culture*, Simon & Schuster, New York, 1982.

Cerjan, Paul, Lt. GEN., USA, Personal Communication, Washington, D.C., 1994.

Deming, W. Edwards, *Out of the Crisis*, MIT Press, Cambridge, 1986.

Deming, W. Edwards, *The New Economics*, MIT Press, Cambridge, MA, 1993.

De Geus, Arie, *The Living Company: Habits for Survival in a Turbulent Business Environment*, Harvard Business School Press, Boston, 1997.

Dougherty, Andrew, COL., Personal Communication with the author, Washington, D.C., 1990.

Marshall, George C. "Report to the Secretary of War: Biennial Report of the Chief of Staff of the U.S. Army," July 1, 1943 – June 30, 1945.

McPhee, John, *La Place de la Concorde Suisse*, Farrar, Straus and Giroux, New York, 1983.

Sagan, Carl, *Cosmos*, Ballantine Books, New York, 1980.

Schwartz, Peter, *The Art of the Long View*, Doubleday, New York, 1991.

Senge, Peter M. *The Fifth Discipline: The Art and Practice of The Learning Organization*, Bantam Doubleday, New York, 1990.

SETI, http://www.astrobio.net/news/modules.php?op=modload&name=News&file=article&sid=1745, 2006.

Taylor, Charles W., *Alternative World Scenarios for Strategic Planning*, U.S. Army War College, Carlisle, 1990 Edition.

Tzu, Sun, *The Art of War*, Translated by Samuel B. Griffith, Oxford University Press, Oxford, 1963.

About the Author

D r. Sheila R. Ronis is Director of the MBA/MSSL Programs at Walsh College in Troy, Michigan. She is also President of The University Group, Inc., a management consulting firm and think tank specializing in strategic management, visioning, national security and public policy. In 2005, she chaired at the Industrial College of the Armed Forces the Army's Eisenhower National Security Series Conference, "The State of the U.S. Industrial Base: National Security Implications in a World of Globalization." The *Proceedings* of that conference, which Dr. Ronis co-edited with Dr. Lynne Thompson was published by the National Defense University Press in April, 2006.

The auto industry, telecommunications, defense and national security have been at the center of her work for thirty-five years in industry, government and academia. Through The University Group, she has worked with many organizations; public, private, large, small, profit and nonprofit. These include: The U.S. House of Representatives, General Motors Corporation, Ford Motor Company, the Department of Defense, the Department of Energy, the Federal Laboratory Consortium For Technology Transfer, U.S. Institute of Peace, USAID, AT&T, USCAR, the Interstate Commerce Commission, the Institute for National Strategic Studies at the National Defense University, the National Academy of Sciences, and The State Council of The People's Republic of China.

Recently, Dr. Ronis was asked to chair the Vision and Guiding Principles Working Group of the Project on National Security Reform under the leadership of the Honorable James R. Locher, III.